INDRA NOOYI
A Biography

INDRA NOOYI
A Biography

Annapoorna

ISBN : 9788170289722

Ist Edition : 2011, Reprint 5th Edition : 2015

© Rajpal & Sons

INDRA NOOYI (A Biography) by Annapoorna

RAJPAL & SONS

1590, Madarsa Road, Kashmere Gate, Delhi-110006
Phone : 011-23869812, 23865483, Fax : 011-23867791
website : www.rajpalpublishing.com
e-mail : sales@rajpalpublishing.com
www.facebook.com/rajpalandsons

CONTENTS

Prologue

On 28 October, 1955, newspapers reported the news of an Icelandic author, Haldor Kiljan Laxness, winning the Nobel Prize for literature. He had written his first novel at the age of seventeen. That same day, in the United States of America, a couple named William and Mary had just had a son, William H. Gates, better known today as Bill Gates. And across the world, the University of Madras in India was celebrating its centenary. This day of celebrations and recognitions was an apt birthday for a girl who would only add to its glory. Born into the Krishnamurthy family in 1955, the little girl was named Indra-a prophetic name, the name of the Hindu King of gods, the bearer of lightening, a colourful king whose royal title did not stand in the way of him occasionally landing in soups of varying depths.

What does it take to make Indra Nooyi? While her parents would perhaps say the answer is the right genes, Ms Nooyi herself in an address at her alma mater, IIM Calcutta, replied, "Candidness, confidence, boundless energy, unending hope and an energizing vision encapsulated in a compassionate world view."

Singer, mother, wife, daughter, but best known for being CEO of PepsiCo, Indra Nooyi gives new meaning to the term 'first among equals'.

Our praise of the feet of the Great Lord fills
the streets everywhere. You ought to have lost the sense
of the self in heaving breath. How is it, unaffected, you
remain in bed, lost in cosy sleep?

— Opening verse of "Tiruvempavai" —

1

A TRADITIONAL UPBRINGING

A little girl in two plaits, a skirt and a blouse wearily eyed the two buckets of water that were hers. Her eyes were heavy with sleep but she knew she would have to jump into action pretty soon.

Dawn was about to break. She could hear the neighbourhood women sprinkling water at their doorsteps, cleaning the area to make *kolams* or floor paintings—beautiful designs made with rice flour. *Kolams* were and still are made outside every home in south India, rich or poor. In her neighbourhood too, the women would sprinkle water just outside their thresholds, sweep away the extra water and, pinching some rice flour between their thumb and index finger, draw lines in the shape of a lotus or conch or other such designs. These auspicious lines that augur prosperity for the home also provide food for ants and other small insects. As it was the festive season of Navratri, the *kolams* were even larger than usual, often decorated with flowers and lamps. Outside this little girl's house too was a beautiful *kolam* her mother had made just that morning while she still rubbed sleep from her young eyes.

Not everybody could afford two buckets of water to bathe in because the water supply had a tendency to stop erratically. On a good day, the municipal water supply was turned on for two hours in the morning, and the household had devised ways to fill up the maximum number of containers. The Tamil Brahmin, known for his intelligence, applied all of his skills to the pursuit, and many of the houses in the neighbourhood had pipes attached to all the taps with containers at various levels, planned such that the maximum amount of water was collected in huge drums and every available bucket. Today, the water was flowing in the taps between three and five in the morning, though this schedule could change at any minute.

The Krishnamurthy household had arrived at a system of water management whereby each member of the family was allocated two buckets of water for the day, or until the water came next. Contemplating her two buckets, Indra heard her grandfather clearing his throat and muttering a mantra under his breath. That meant he was through with his morning ablutions and bath. Then she heard him mix his coffee.

Every household in south India has a father or grandfather

brought up with the belief that the early hours of the morning are best spent on study. In those days, no one thought of organising a children's union or else all children would have ganged up, ready even to murder if only they could be allowed to linger in bed just a little longer. But no, at the crack of dawn the household buzzed with activity as if there were no tomorrow and the students of the house were expected to be immersed in their studies.

And so Indra Krishnamurthy too was awake, managing her day's water ration and trying to get dressed before her grandfather came upon her. The smell of roasted coffee beans wafted through the air mingling with the equally strong perfume of jasmine flowers that were freshly bought for the morning prayers. Tamilians are coffee drinkers and like to use what is called a 'tumbler' and a davara. A tumbler is a stainless steel glass while a davara is a kind of cup that serves as a saucer for the glass. Tamilians are adept at pouring the coffee from the glass into the davara from a great height in order to cool it and build up a froth. In Indra's house too, even as she stood there eyeing her buckets, her grandfather was cooling his coffee and drinking the hot liquid without allowing the glass to touch his lips.

Her mother in the adjoining room, like most Tamilian women, was twirling a strand of jasmine flowers around her thick, long plait. Some women would buy heaps of jasmine buds and string them together at home. Their fragrance would fill the house, particularly the puja or the prayer room, gleaming with its polished idols of gods and family deities. Indra's mother had begun her morning by offering flowers to the gods, after which the flowers and strands would be distributed among the women of the house. And all this activity before five in the morning!

Outside the house, the city was coming to life, bustling, tinkling and chiming to meet the new day. Temple bells were ringing and middle-aged men reciting Sanskrit shlokas or verses, walked barefoot to the nearby temple, their foreheads smeared with sandal paste and ash depicting their caste.

Inside the house Indra's mother bustled around, all bathed and ready in a Kanjeevaram silk sari worn from repeated washes. Her hair, still wet from her bath, was loosely tied with a thin white towel at the nape of her neck. In the middle of her forehead was a dot of *kumkum,* the bright crimson powder that symbolizes marriage, and below it, a smear of the sacred ash, *vibhuti.* Indra would be given some *vibhuti* after her bath as well—a small ritual she always looked forward to. She liked how her face looked with the grey smear— Indian, attractive, and much like her mother's.

•

The Krishnamurthy family home stood in the heart of the capital city of Madras, now Chennai, in an area known as T Nagar. It was a busy area, full of shops selling everything from pins to gold ornaments and it was also home to the middle class Brahmins and the nouveau riche of Chennai. Some film actors, including the famous Sivaji Ganesan, lived in this area. Nearby, on GN Chetty Road, was the Krishnamurthy house, between what was once known as the Sun Theatre and Panagal Park.

On GN Chetty Road was another great attraction and

landmark for all Tamilians—the Vani Mahal. Owned by the Tyaga Brahma Gana Sabha, one of the oldest sabhas (organizations for the arts) in the city, it was a great cultural hub. Indra's favourite actor and comedian, Tamil theatre's superstar Nagesh, had made his debut here, and Waheeda Rehman, well-known Hindi cinema actor, had presented her maiden dance performance here long before she appeared in films. The Chief Minister of Tamil Nadu, Jayalalitha, who was formerly a well-known actor in Tamil films, gave one of her earliest dance recitals here as well. Many great stalwarts have performed at Vani Mahal and even today it continues to be a hub of classical music and art. It also often serves as a venue for wedding receptions. Renovated three years ago, it was transformed into one of the city's finest auditoriums.

Mylapore, a neighbouring area, was more affluent and not as badly off—water-wise—as T. Nagar in those days, but it soon came to share the same dry fate. Today, however, with the Kauveri river waters being diverted to Chennai, and with water harvesting in many houses, the water problem is not as acute.

It is in the well-to-do neighbourhood of Mylapore that Indra, who sat gazing at her two buckets of water, would about forty years later buy a house in its most posh colony, Poes Garden. But whether knowing this would have helped her while she was being rationed water and woken up in the early hours of the morning, one cannot tell!

●

Although the young Indra's schedule was usually quite full of household chores, the last week had been particularly hectic because of Navaratri, also known as Dussehra in the north, the nine-day festival celebrated primarily by women. It was customary in Tamil Nadu for women or girls to visit their friends and invite other women to visit them during those nine days. A typical practice of this festival is arranging dolls known as *golu* dolls on several steps in a corner of the house. Women and young girls are then invited to sit facing them. Generally those who sing (and in Tamil Nadu most women sing!) render classical Carnatic ragas. Indra and her sister Chandrika being good at it would sing everywhere they went. Then they would enjoy the *sundal,* a preparation of various lentils, flavoured with coconut and lemon. The women would also be given the auspicious *vethalai pakku,* which contained *kumkum* with betel leaf and perhaps a blouse piece or cosmetic items. The girls would collect their gifts and go on to the next house all dolled up in *pattu pavadais* (long silk skirts). On other days, they would stay at home to receive visitors and offer them *vethalai pakku.*

Since Indra's mother felt such traditions were as important as studies, she took her daughters out everywhere and also had them in full attendance when people came home. Now it was time to get dressed and Indra was required to hurry. But instead of hurrying up, Indra was addressing a deeply Shakespearean question: 'To bathe or not to bathe'. The question was of course futile because obviously she had to bathe, yet the task of apportioning water for the whole day led to deep thoughts. Her sister Chandrika had already had a bath. So had the rest of her family -- her mother, her grandfather and her brother. Her father, as was the case most often, was out of town. He would probably be coming back that night. Her green frock with its white and green piping, her school uniform that she had ironed the evening before, was by her bed and urging her to decide quickly.

Indra could hear her mother tap the lid of the coffee filter. When the coffee decoction did not percolate fast enough, a little tap on the head of the coffee filter did the trick by galvanizing the powder into giving the decoction space to trickle down. This tap was generally for the second round of decoction. It galvanized Indra too and she quickly got up to get ready.

Her school, one of the best and among the oldest schools of Chennai, was located on Thyagaraya Road. Run by the Franciscan Missionaries of Mary, The Holy Angels Anglo Indian Higher Secondary School, as it was known then, is today known simply as Holy Angels Convent. School started at half past eight and they would leave home just before eight. Indra was ready to start studying right away so she could get at least two hours of work done before leaving. She would be home by four in the evening because school got over by quarter past three.

She knew how it would be in the evening. The silhouette of her grandfather would be visible from the gate as he paced up and down the house waiting for them to get back from school. Suddenly she remembered that it was the first of the new month and her little hands reaching for her buckets trembled slightly in nervous anticipation.

Learning a man secures in one birth will secure his well-being in seven.

— *Tirukural* —

2

A ROLE MODEL FOR INDRA

It was on the first day of the month that Indra received her monthly report card at school. Her stern grandfather would be waiting to examine it and so it was in her interest to be in his good books that morning.

Sure enough Narayana Sharma, retired district judge well known in Chennai, was pleased to see his granddaughter poring over her books. He believed academics alone would hold a human being in a position of strength, and he was not alone in thinking so. To this day, the state of Tamil Nadu continues to be an academically and intellectually inclined one and Shantha, Indra's mother, too swore by the importance of excelling at academics for success in life.

"In those days," Indra reminisced, "any Tamil Brahmin did that. The entire family focused on grades. When parents got together, all they discussed was the report cards of their children. They would ask, 'So how is your child doing?', 'What rank?' That was growing up in the '50s and '60s. As long as you got good grades you were okay. If you did not get good grades you were not worth it. In our school system, we used to get report cards every month. Thirty kids in every class and every month we got a rank. The report card came on the 30th of every month and my grandfather would stand at the door waiting for it." Facetiously, Indra continues describing what propelled her to work hard at school, "If you didn't rank in the first three, you might want to kill yourself on the way back home because he was going to kill you. So those were your two choices -- killed by your grandfather or jump before a moving bus. When you have that sort of a goal to make all the time, you must work your tail off. I just can't remember a time when I did not work my tail off."

There was additional pressure in the form of Indra's elder sister Chandrika who always excelled in her studies. Indra says, "You always tend to look at your sister. How can she do so well and you cannot? She came first and you, only third. Holy cow, let me go back and work." Chandrika was two years senior to Indra in school, and their peer group remembers Chandrika as the "intelligent" one and Indra as the quiet one.

All work and no play did not make Indra a dull girl. "I wanted to play cricket. I wanted to be a rock star. But my grandfather would always say, 'You are going to study hard.' And so it was I studied all my life." Her mother too expected her to excel. "It was no fun sometimes, really awful," she recalls. "If you came home with 95 in geography, you had to study geography for the next two weeks. My mother would cry if you didn't get 100 in math."

At Holy Angels where the girls studied, the standard of math and science was a little higher since they followed the Anglo Indian Higher Secondary system, which was a take off from the 'O' levels of Cambridge. So whenever students from the school joined pre-University, they always had an edge over students from other schools. At that time, schools were shifting from the ICSC system of examination to Central and State Boards. Holy Angels had opted for the AIHS (Anglo Indian Higher Secondary) system.

Education wasn't the single most important aspect of life in the Krishnamurthy household alone, it was the state-wide obsession of the entire Tamil Nadu! In fact, most south Indian states emphasized education for women as well as men, and the triumph of this equality can be seen in the achievements of stalwarts like world-renowned classical singer MS Subbulakshmi, the poet Sarojini Naidu and the dancer Rukmini Devi Arundale. Some of the best doctors, academicians and intellectuals in south India have been women. There were also many institutions for the education of girls.

Shantha had made a number of sacrifices to ensure her daughters received the best education possible. Her husband, Indra's father Krishnamurthy, worked in the State Bank of Hyderabad. At the time of her marriage, Shantha was faced with a choice-to travel with her husband or live in her father-in-law's house on 88 GN Chetty Road in Mambalam. Shantha chose to live in Chennai to secure quality education for her future children-that's how forward thinking she was. After her two girls, Shantha's son Narayanan, or Nandu, was born almost twelve years later. She focused on her children and believed that more is wrought by prayer than the world dreams of. She prayed four to five hours everyday and for the rest concentrated on keeping her home immaculate.

Indra and her siblings have always seen the world through the prism of their mother's faith and beliefs, with Indra often calling the devout Hindu Brahmin the guiding light in her life. "Our house had a very large temple room, and my mother used to pray three or four hours every morning. So the house was a deeply religious house, and every occasion of life and death was observed with great care and exacting standards."

Shantha gave Chandrika, Indra and Narayanan as full a life as possible. Apart from the rigorous education, Indra also remembers her as often enjoying Tamil movies with the three of them. One of Indra's favourite actors was Nagesh, a well loved comedian of the early sixties and seventies. Those were the days when television had not yet come to India, so movies used to be seen only in theatres and going to the cinema was an event.

But it was not only while studying and during movies that Shantha and her children spent quality time together. There was a whole host of activities Shantha had devised to ensure that the time she devoted to her children was always constructive.

According to Indra, one of the secrets behind her unparalleled desire for success is that while she and her siblings were growing up, their mother would have them deliver a post-prandial speech every night on topics like what they wanted to be, "...whether it was the president of India, prime minister... or chief minister of a state." Following each of her children's speeches, she would cast her vote for the winner, the reward being a small piece of chocolate. Perhaps these were simple childhood games to them at the time, but today Indra recognizes the role they played in slowly building her confidence and understandably refers to her mother as one of her "greatest role models".

Shantha could not imagine anything that her children, or for that matter she, could not do. It still makes her smile whenever she hears her famous daughter Indra say at interviews, "Actually I think my mother wished she was the prime minister of the country." However, even while she instilled in them great ambitions to go beyond their limited world, she also inculcated in them an understanding of the traditions of south Indian life. Her ambition was consuming and she passed that fire to her children. And yet she also wished as earnestly that her daughters get married and have children.

Looking back on those years of her life Indra says, "My mother was the constant force and I think she always wished she were the prime minister of this country. She is a real go-getter. She passed on her ambition and she always said to us—she was an interesting study in contrasts—'I want to get you married when you are eighteen, and make sure you aspire to be the prime minister'. We never figured out where she came from. I think my father, my grandfather, all said, 'Our granddaughters are going to be whatever they want to be'. So my mother really did not have this get-them-married-by-eighteen option, although she kept on threatening us with that."

"Amma, make up your mind," they would say, but Shantha could never think of compromising one aspect of life for another. This unwillingness to give up any aspect of life led to a lot of very heated discussions. But it contributed to turning her daughters into ideal women—good managers at home and at work.

Achieving this had not been easy. Shantha lived in the heart of the traditional city of Chennai, where no sooner had one's daughter finished school than all that the mothers talked of was the jewellery they were making for them and which bachelor was most eligible and whether their horoscopes would match. Call it arrogance, but Shantha knew her daughters were not like the typical girls of the neighbourhood. She did not intend for them to marry just any rich boy and waste their life having children, boiling milk and buying blouse pieces at Luz, the favourite shopping centre of most women. Yet, she knew her girls had to get married one day. Did they not say the more you delay, the less likely you are to find a match in the same community and from a good family? Every day, some lady or other, acquaintances near and distant, announced the engagement of their daughters, and some even pointedly asked, "So what about Chandrika? You have two of them. If you delay the first one's wedding, the second will get too delayed...."

At home, her husband and father-in-law did not seem to understand. Sometimes Shantha was happy they were so strong. At other times she was worried because everybody said it was a wife's duty to pressurize her husband. The only way in which she could vent her frustration was to admonish the girls themselves. Says Indra, "She threatened us by saying that all kinds of things will happen. But at the end of the day, you know, deep down inside, I think she said, 'this is what I would really like to do. But that is really what they want to do. And let me not stop them'. Really, it was difficult. But somehow I think the family pulled together and said 'let them do it'. But just do not forget the family, do not forget the heritage, do not forget where you come from, just live life consistent with that."

It wasn't only Indra's home—Chennai on the whole was a conservative city. It was still inward looking. Be it the clothes that the women wore, which was usually just the chaste sari, or the fact that few ever cut their hair short or the portrayal of women in films, the attitude was very protective. The Tamil Brahmins, particularly of those days, had very clear ideas on what was 'good' and what was 'bad'. Perhaps it was a fear of the unknown or the fear of losing their identity that had them drawing deep boundaries between the two. One telling comment of Indra brings back the environment that prevailed in Chennai at that time: "When I was growing up in India, we tended to draw conclusions too quickly and it was all in black and white. The thing I learned in my time at Yale was that shades of grey predominate. You need to think about an issue in its full glory and richness before you jump to a conclusion, so I came (to Yale) an intelligent person and left an educated person."

The girls were not sure how life would turn out. But somehow, despite all of their mother's worries, both Indra and Chandrika's path in life turned out to be the ideal one.

Indra often wonders, "Where I was born, the way I was brought up, the last thing I expected was to be where I am. So you just can't tell!"

To rule the realms and make the laws
We have risen;
Nor shall it be said that woman lags behind man in
the
knowledge that he attaineth.
Dance the Kummi1, beat the measure
Let this land of the Tamils ring with our dance.
For now we are rid of all evil shades;
We have seen the Good

— *Subramaniya Bharathi in The 'Kummi' of Women's Freedom* —

3

THE COLLEGE YEARS

Sa, sa, sa, sa, re, re re, re, ga, ga, ga, ga... Indra and Chandrika dwelled on one note after another, rigorously learning the Carnatic classical singing style throughout school and college. Music was an important part of the average Tamilian's life, especially in T Nagar with the popular venue for performance, Vani Mahal, being close by. Indra's family took a particular interest in music and they often found themselves at the Mahal, enjoying performances by various singers and later dissecting them, the ragas and modifications. Music was in Indra's blood. Her aunt Aruna Sairam is a noted singer, and this gave the sisters an almost intuitive understanding of and love for the art form. Indra was equally at home practising a *varnam* or *keertanai* in Carnatic music.

Together, the sisters and Shantha would attend music concerts and often challenge each other to identify the raga as soon as the singer had begun. Indra of course excelled at the game, which along with teaching her about Indian music also helped her imbibe its spiritual aspects. Even today, Indra tries to attend the annual music concert in Chennai held every December and has been known to break into song even in a corporate setting!

If there was emphasis on Carnatic music in the home, western music came to Indra through school and later the college she joined—Madras Christian College, one of the best educational institutions of Chennai that ranked almost as high as the illustrious Indian Institute of Technology (IIT) not only in terms of its sylvan surroundings but also the quality and standard of education it imparted.

It was in 1972 that Indra joined MCC for her Pre-University (PUC), going on to complete her Bachelors in Physics, Chemistry and Mathematics. Earlier the College had been for men only and had started accepting women students around the time Indra joined. That Indra should have been allowed to go to MCC is significant. At the time, most girls went to all-girls colleges like Stella Maris, Ethiraj or Queen Mary's. But some science subjects like Chemistry were not offered at these colleges. So that left few options and Indra ended up at MCC. Although her parents considered MCC "safe" for their daughter, it was nevertheless a step forward for the conservative family from Chennai to send its daughters to the outskirts of the city to study in a co-educational college. More than open mindedness, it shows the determination of the family to provide their children with the best possible education. Perhaps going to a co-educational institution during a period when co-education was still gaining acceptance was one of the reasons Indra learnt to stand as an equal among equals and storm a male bastion in later years.

The college was a long train ride away in Tambaram. Although the gate leading into the college is just outside the station, it is still a substantial walk from the college building. This long commute and hectic study schedule did not deter the sisters from participating in other activities. Indra became part of an all-girls rock band, playing the electric guitar and singing. The band was often called upon to perform and some of their favourite numbers included the Beatles and Harry Belafonte. A singer whom Indra and her band mates especially admired was Usha Uthup. Another Saivite Tamilian, Usha, who began her career as Usha Iyer, had caught the fancy of Indra's peer group not only because she was among the first Indian women to sing western pop but because she did so wearing a sari!

Clothes were of great importance in the south India of those times. Girls after a certain age wore only saris. "Punjabi suits", as the salwar kameez was often referred to, were still not common. Trousers and jeans were what every young girl looked at longingly, which parents rarely allowed. When Usha Uthup began singing in night clubs wearing a sari, parents pointed her out to their daughters as the ideal south Indian girl. Indra's own wardrobe consisted mainly of saris and later when she was in the US buying clothes before an interview, she said, "I never looked at skirts because I had not shown my legs before. To wear skirts would be to expose my legs, so I looked only at trousers."

Along with music, both girls also went to the Alliance Francaise to learn to speak (and even sing!) in French. The Alliance Francaise was one of the first institutions teaching a foreign language in India. Most educated families with aspirations sent their children, particularly daughters, there. German and French were the only two foreign languages that were being taught at institutions in India at the time and French was the more popular choice perhaps because it was more widely spoken around the world than German.

And so we have a young Indra Krishnamurthy, still many years away from acquiring her now world famous name. A sprightly, intelligent young girl, charged up to take life head on. The ambition aroused in Indra by her mother prompted her to find opportunities for herself everywhere. In college there was once a situation when a department magazine could not be brought out due to lack of funds. It was generally left to the boys to go out and meet people to request sponsorships. This time as well, a group of students went into town to visit business houses. One of the young men in the group was Dr VJ Philip who later went on to become the principal of MCC. In this group of young men, Philip remembers, was one single girl-Indra Krishnamurthy-standing out for her confidence.

Looking back at incidents such as these, one gets a sense of how much of her strong willed, confident personality Indra had built by that time. Her friends and peers describe her then as bubbly, confident, enthusiastic and easy to get along with. They also often identify a trait that Indra herself thinks was one of the things her family taught her, which is that she never left a job halfway. As she said in an interview, "One of the things my parents and my grandfather taught me was when you do a job you have got to do it better than everybody else. Simple. You cannot let anybody down. I will tell you, today at PepsiCo if I am given a job, people who work with me and people I work for will tell you that even if Indra is dying she will make sure the job gets done because I just don't know any other way to work."

Dr VJ Philip says the same about her. Philip and Indra joined college at the same time, in 1972. He was a postgraduate student while she was in her first year. By the time she got to her final year, he had completed his master's and joined the college as a lecturer. "So," he says with a smile, "I was both her classmate and professor!" Reminiscing about the money collection drive for the college magazine, Dr Philip remembers, "It was the early seventies and she was the only girl ready to help us. Unlike other girls, she used to run with us to catch buses and trains. We would run from one company to another. She was good at leading a group and played a very important role in organizing events. I could see her leadership qualities even then. No other girl would take the initiative of going to the city to get advertisements."

He candidly admits she wasn't an extraordinarily brilliant student of Chemistry. "Her interests didn't lie in the subject; there were many students better than her. But she stood out in class because of her all-round personality. She was excellent in cultural activities like singing, strumming a guitar or leading a band. She had her own music group, and participated in dramatics. There was nothing she hadn't done in college."

Indra was also known for speaking her mind and standing

up for what she believed in. Philip recounts an incident concerning a particularly tough test paper that had been set for her class by one of the professors. Indra, who was then in the first year, got her class to solve it and then barged into the lecturer's room to show him why everybody had performed badly. Far from being reprimanded, "we had a re-test," says Philip with a smile, marvelling at the lengths to which Indra would go to stand for what she believed in.

Dr R Wilfred Sugumar, head of the Department of Chemistry at MCC, was also Indra's classmate from 1972-1974. He recalls her various achievements and speaks of her highly. "She had a drama group that went to north India for a competition and came back with a prize. She was that kind of person; she never accepted defeat." Sugumar also remembers that though she was from a fairly well-to-do family, she was "down-to-earth and friendly."

He may have always got more marks than her in Chemistry, but his memories of Indra go beyond the academic. "I used to be next to her in the lab and we were supposed to do experiments together. Coming from a small town, I was very shy and felt embarrassed standing next to a girl. She knew my discomfort and used to bully and tease me a lot. She played a lot of pranks on me," recalls Sugumar fondly.

Yet another extra-curricular activity Indra was involved in was cricket! The young girl was a successful addition to the women's cricket team and clearly brought her sportsperson's spirit from the field to every aspect of her life.

Both Dr. Philip and Dr. Sugumar, as well as most of Indra's other friends and college mates, knew she was destined for greatness. But perhaps even they could not have imagined just how great she would be! The Madras Christian College that had produced such eminent personalities as businessman TT Krishnamachari, diplomat KPS Menon, scientist Dr. Raja Ramanna and Chief Election Commissioner TN Seshan, created yet another public personality India can be proud of.

But how did Indra evolve into one of the world's most successful businesswomen? After her graduation in 1974, like many of the other girls in her class, she too was expected to take on teaching or research. But her goals were different. Although she was a fairly good science student, her various extra-curricular activities suggested that her real talents were her people skills, her strong and confident personality, her ability to work tirelessly towards a goal and most of all, her endless energy and motivation to win and be the best at whatever she was doing. These abilities, Indra realized, would be wasted as a teacher or researcher.

It's been a hard day's night, and
I've been working like a dog,

It's been a hard day's night,
I should be sleeping like a log

— *The Beatles* —

4

A REVOLUTIONARY DECISION

Indra sat at home one evening, a cup of filtered coffee balanced on a book beside her, her long cotton skirt splayed across the bed. She had recently graduated from MCC and now had an important decision to make. She sat under the slowly revolving fan, turning over the options in her mind. Glancing at her guitar lying across the bed, she ruefully thought of how her days of being a rock star were over. Images of her carefree college days came to mind like a slideshow. There she was performing with her guitar on stage, and there gathering with her group debating on what to sing...

On the coffee table beside her, a large radio sat with its volume turned down low. Indra had an extensive collection of records by some of her favourite bands, but the evenings belonged to the 'Forces Request' programme on radio. The room was filling with the haunting sounds of Harry Belafonte singing...

> *Work all night on a drink a' rum*
>
> *Daylight come and me wan' go home*
>
> *Stack banana till de mornin' come*
>
> *Daylight come and me wan' go home*

Indra's mind was restless and she'd thought that the song would help her relax but it wasn't helping. How was she to know that the decision she was about to take in that room would one day, twenty-seven years later, have her hosting an event for the employees of PepsiCo, one of the world's largest companies, where she would not only meet the singer Harry Belafonte but also sing that very same song along with him!

The story goes that at the function Indra Nooyi stood up to introduce guest speaker Harry Belafonte and make her official speech. Then serving as Pepsi's Chief Financial Officer, she praised the company's strides in creating a more diverse workplace but challenged it not to rest on its laurels. Then she broke from the script and led more than a hundred employees in an impromptu sing-along of the entertainer's famous song Day-O. Suddenly, the corporate tone of the evening was replaced with a magical spirit that brought the CFO closer to her entire team.

Back in the present, Indra had arrived at a decision.

Management was the field, she realized, which would make the best use of her varied skills. Her elder sister,

Chandrika, had enrolled in the Indian Institute of Management (IIM), Ahmedabad, the previous year and within a few weeks, Indra too had enrolled herself for the PGDBA (Post Graduate Diploma in Business Administration) programme at IIM Calcutta.

Indra's family did not oppose her decision but they did wonder why an intelligent girl like her should choose to study something like management. And that too, in marketing. Wasn't marketing meant for boys? Engineering or medicine they could understand, but marketing? Even so, the girls had taken their decisions and the family stood by them.

The family had also not been too surprised when Indra got accepted into the Institute. After all, Chandrika too had been accepted only the previous year. But it had been difficult for the family to let their youngest daughter leave Chennai. The entire extended family came to bid Indra farewell, and each member gave her a different piece of advice. "Don't stay out after dark," "Be suspicious of people who are too nice to you," "Write every day". There were endless instructions and also phone numbers of relatives—close and distant— living in Calcutta. But the family knew Calcutta was a safe place for women and that Indra would work hard and do her best.

Sending both her daughters away to stay in a hostel had been difficult for Shantha but her burning ambition for them overshadowed her sadness.

•

Indra's arrival at IIMC in 1976 set no major bells ringing.

She was one of the youngest students in her class. The campus which had recently moved location was now at Joka and Indra's was the first batch to study there. Overall, hers was only the eleventh batch. Traditions had not yet developed. Her name does not feature in the honour rolls of her batch. Her batch had 122 students. Of these, only six were women. While all the students of the IIMs were expected to find the secret to make the world a more profitable place, here as in MCC, no one expected this easy-going south Indian girl to scale such dizzying heights.

Professor Ranjan Das who studied at IIM Ahmedabad around the same time recalls that the teachers in those days were trained in the US, and all the companies discussed and studied in B-schools were largely American. And there weren't many who wanted to go to a B-school. "There was no craze for an MBA education in those days. I would say that people who went for an MBA education in those days were really frontrunners. They looked at the world quite differently. I would say they were really thinking ahead of the times. And today when I see, after thirty years, the kind of people who are joining MBA education, it's clear that they were people who thought about their career positively." Indra of course was a frontrunner, though few recognized it at the time.

At the IIM, Indra was well loved amongst her classmates. Many of the professors felt that she stood out. She began showing some signs of her eventual choice of career. Theory was not her favourite topic of study. As Anindya Sen, now the Dean of IIMC says, "Indra had a knack for marketing and had taken up courses like international marketing, consumer behaviour, sales management etc. Her grades were better in marketing-related subjects."

Indra's popularity among her co-students is evident from the various anecdotes they narrate about her. A batch mate, Tushar Basu, now director of Analytic Consultants, remembers her as "hardworking, assertive, friendly and helpful, all at the same time. As at MCC, it was not just academics that interested her. She was also active in extra-curricular activities like music, cricket and table tennis."

Goutam Ghosh, a business management teacher and a fellow batch mate, recollects the first time he met Indra one evening over a cup of tea, immediately after the batch met for the first time. "I was amazed to see such a young girl with so much confidence."

Nabendu Gupta, who was a year junior to her and now runs a consulting firm, remembers her as a tough table tennis opponent who was aggressive and ambitious.

The teaching philosophy at the IIMs has changed over the years. Instead of focusing purely on academics as they once did, today the advice given to new students is that academic excellence is not enough nor the sole criterion of success. An all-rounder has a greater chance to make it, and a common example quoted is that of Indra Krishnamurthy Nooyi.

Nearly thirty years after graduating from IIM, Indra returned to address the students. Dean Anindya Sen introduced her as a student who was not on the honour rolls of the college, yet one of its best known graduates—a statement greeted with thundering applause. In her speech, Indra would acknowledge the contribution of the Institute in making her a better people manager and enabling her success. So inspiring was her talk that a second-year student, Abhishek Saha, said in an interview, "I think the floodgates are about to open. Just like the '90s saw a whole lot of technopreneurs rising, we are waiting for more presidents, CFOs, CEOs in old world economies, in old world companies just waiting to rise. More Indians, more IIM Calcuttans."

Going back to the days when Indra was still a fresh graduate of the IIM, we see her a bit unsure about what to do next. Getting a job was the obvious next step, though others advised her to try and go abroad right away. The insistent clamour in the guise of friendly advice to get her daughters married was ringing in Shantha's ears.

What was Indra to do next?

"Now, here, you see, it takes all the running
you can do, to keep in the same place.
If you want to get somewhere else, you must run at
least twice as fast as that!"

— *Alice in Wonderland, Lewis Carroll* —

5

LOOKING WEST

Indra sat on the sands of Marina Beach, eating *thenga-manga-sundal,* a Chennai speciality made of boiled lentils, coconut and raw mangoes. The sun was setting and the sky was turning a deep shade of orange. The sea looked particularly lovely, as if it had been set aflame. Much like the mind of the young woman silhouetted against it.

It was a place Indra had often visited with her parents. On moonlit nights, the family had enjoyed many tranquil moments on this, one of south India's most beautiful beaches, known for its twelve kilometre long shoreline and large expanses of clean sand. Indra stood up, dusted the sand off her kurta, and started to walk along the shore. In the distance, she could see the tall flagpost of Fort St. George. The Bay of Bengal glittered orange and silver, a strong wind whipping her hair into her eyes. She could not help thinking that, like the sea, her thoughts too were riding through rough weather.

Indra's heart hurt at the thought of leaving this beach behind, this beach where she and Chandrika had played as children, collected numerous shells and chased the waves. She remembered holding her father's hand as he led her to the famous Cassata ice cream stand. But she would have to leave it all behind.

The coveted IIM degree now in hand, she had started getting several lucrative job offers. Chandrika had left for Beirut for a job with Citibank shortly after graduating from IIM Ahmedabad, and her departure had not been easy on the family. "There was a lot of opposition at home from the elders to letting Chandrika go to Beirut then," Krishnamurthy, her father, says. Indra explains this hesitation. "It was unheard of for a good, conservative, south Indian Brahmin girl to do this. It would make her an absolutely unmarriageable commodity after that."

Her parents didn't know then that Indra too had arrived at the decision to go abroad to study.

After graduating from IIMC Indra's first job was with Tootal, a British textile company founded in Manchester in 1799, with extensive holdings in India. After that, she was hired as a brand manager at the Bombay offices of Johnson & Johnson, the personal care products maker. She was given the Stayfree account, which might have proved a major challenge for even an experienced marketing executive. The line had just been introduced in the market and it was a struggle to create for it a distinctive identity. "It was a fascinating experience because you couldn't advertise personal protection in India," she later recalled in an interview with the 'Financial Times'.

From J&J, Indra moved to the textile firm, Mettur Beardsell Ltd. Her third professional switch led to many raised eyebrows. In conservative Tamil Nadu, once you got a job, you stuck to it for life, permanently holding your position armed with loyalty and a deep sense of gratitude. Many of the Krishnamurthys' relatives and neighbours wondered, "Why is she moving jobs so quickly? Money is not everything. For a few thousand rupees more why give up a reputed company?"

For a twenty three-year-old, such remarks were disconcerting. As Indra later said, "The core of the concept of success lies in knowing what you want to do in life and those who have triumphed at figuring out that issue should consider themselves tremendously blessed." She for one knew life could not stop here. Her process of learning had just begun. She had worked with multinationals but was not yet aware of life outside the country. She knew she needed to grow both professionally and personally, and she knew it had to be done outside the protected environment of her hometown. So despite her initial successes, Indra began to feel she would stagnate if she continued like this, that perhaps she was under-prepared for the higher echelons of business success. Also, she was determined to study in the United States, where she felt all the action in her field of interest was. She once said, "I always had this urge, this desire, this passion to settle in the United States." Around the time this passion was turning ripe, a magazine advertisement for the Yale School of Management caught her eye, and she impulsively applied.

At that time, applying to a university abroad meant many walks to the post office, getting the right kind of envelope, weighing the packet, an interminably long wait for a response and other such concerns that are irrelevant today. Indra was not sure what would come of it, but she was not losing much except for the application fee and so she went ahead.

She knew her decision would be met with opposition. She was also not entirely sure how to go about it—how to apply, manage her money and other details. All she was sure of was that she had to learn more, she had to conquer new vistas. Her mother often expressed her doubts about these attempts, which Indra temporarily silenced with the words, "It is only if I get in Amma."

From the day Indra sent in her application, her parents were a bundle of nerves, unsure which fate they preferred— Indra getting admission and achieving her dreams or being denied and continuing to stay at home.

Krishnamurthy's mind was plagued with questions and concerns. Should he send Indra abroad? His heart said he should. But society cautioned him. Indra often heard lines like, "In the west, they have no family values", "It is not at all safe for a young unmarried girl", "All youngsters take to drugs when they go abroad". All this from people who had never gone abroad themselves. Perhaps the most common refrain was, "What will she do studying so much? Ultimately she has to get married!" Even long after Indra had made the decision to go, arguments from well-meaning (and not so well-meaning!) friends and relatives continued. "You don't get vegetarian food there", "It is very cold, Indians cannot manage that weather" and "Once they go there, they never come back".

Shantha took heed of these warnings but also had her own mindset. She was a bundle of contradictions but definitely seemed stronger than her husband. Sending Chandrika had been a tumultuous experience. Shantha remembered how nervous she had been the day she had left, being unable to sleep until Chandrika had reached and called her up. Now Indra wanted to leave too. But then Avvaiyar, the Tamil poetess had said, "Tirai kadalodiyum driviyam thedu," which means "Cross the seas in search of wealth." And Avvaiyar's wisdom is held in great reverence by the Tamil people. So that should be the motto, Shantha decided. Indra should go!

Shantha was not worried about her daughters' safety or their ability to manage in new surroundings. Neither was she worried by the distance. Only one thing worried her. How would she get them married?

Says Indra about that time and her mother's concerns for her marriage, "There were a lot of proposals! But the good news was that my elder sister refused to get married straight away and I couldn't get married until she did, so I had the licence to go off and dream. I asked my parents for permission to study in America and they were so sure that I wouldn't get in or that I wouldn't get a scholarship that they encouraged me to try."

The family members gave each other strength and collectively arrived at the decision that, if selected, Indra should go to Yale. They realized that getting admission into the illustrious university would be no mean achievement and that it would be sad if she had to give up the opportunity of a lifetime. "Still it is tough to send your own daughter," Shantha would tell her husband as they quietly mused over the prospect.

Chandrika being abroad was of great help and yet her feedback about the people, the food and the weather was not always positive.

Indra did not respond to any of these concerns. It had been several weeks and she still hadn't heard from Yale. The Indian Postal Service was notorious for sometimes taking up to several months to deliver international mail. With no certainty either way, she continued her quiet refrain. "Only if I get in Amma..."

But Shantha would not listen. Many questions plagued her mind. How would they manage their lives away from home? Would their going away mean their future would not be in this country? How would she ever find a suitable match for them? Would they ever come back? What would happen to herself and her husband? And what about Narayanan, her youngest son? Shantha believed that her prayers and her children's well being were related, and she began to enter into various agreements and MOUs with the Lord. She would visit one temple if Indra got admission, another if Chandrika got married, would offer so many *vadais* to the Lord if her daughters were safe, and the list went on.

God must have opened a separate register for the Krishnamurthy family. And He or She must have also attended to the file every day, because one fine day Indra received a beautiful letter in a large, thick white envelope that

congratulated her on her admission to the Master's in Public
and Private Management programme at Yale. The year was
1978.

Later, her father Krishnamurthy said, "Once Chandrika
went, there was no looking back. That was what the children
wanted to do. I would console my mother by saying, 'the
candle has to melt to let the light shine. Think of me as
the candle. Someone has to make a sacrifice if the children
are to do well'."

Life affords no higher pleasure than that of
surmounting difficulties, passing from
one step of success to another, forming new
wishes and seeing them gratified.

— *Samuel Johnson* —

6

ARRIVAL AT YALE

As the aircraft took off with a ferocity that matched Indra's surging ambition, her heart did a somersault. She was really leaving! The shores of Marina Beach were far behind her. And several hours from now she too, like numerous successful businesspersons before her, would be walking the tree-lined boulevards of the Yale University campus. In her mind played the refrain, "Hey world, here I come!"

In the ancient Indian epic, *The Ramayana*, when the monkey god Hanuman leapt across the ocean to go to Lanka, the earth, according to the author Valmiki, shook and propelled many of the other monkeys into the air along with some of the trees and creepers. The same force propelled many of Indra's relatives and friends along with her in several cars to the airport. Soon after being launched into the skies, however, all the uprooted trees fell back to the Earth as though with a heavy heart, as Valmiki describes. And so was Indra's farewell—as vivid as this, with the family returning to a now empty house with heavy feet and many a moist eye.

The past week had been hectic, a mad rush in fact, of shopping, packing, short-listing the eatables she could carry. With few readymade and packaged foods available at the time, the family held numerous heated discussions on the topic. Coffee powder was the first to go in. You never know what you get there, they discussed. If it had too much of chicory it would not taste good; it had to be fresh. A long discussion was held by different people on the topic of carrying pickles. Would the oil leak? Was it worth it? How would they pack them? Should they be packed at all? After great thought and deliberation, the pickle plan was abandoned and the family came up with various dry south Indian preparations—*paruppu podi,* a powder made of lentils that is mixed with rice and eaten, as well as some *vadam* and *vathal* that are dried preparations and can be fried and eaten with rice.

The other major topic of discussion was clothes. Indra had saris galore, but warm clothes? Chennai with its tropical climate was hardly the place to buy the heavy woollens that Connecticut's bitter winter demanded. So a few items were bought from Calcutta and the rest Indra would have to buy after reaching Yale. The one thing she had plenty of were thermals—thick, ugly grey and white layers that an old aunt advised her to "wear under your saris." They did not really go with Indra's sense of style, nor did she know if she'd be able to wear saris in the winter, but carry them she did, influenced at last by the numerous intense discussions on Connecticut and its bone chilling winters.

The other important point on the agenda as preparation for her departure was visits to different temples where the Krishnamurthy family prayed for Indra's future to be safe and bright. There were both quick prayer trips as well as elaborate sessions that required prior preparation of *prasad* (offerings) and ornate Kanjeevaram saris.

Finally, with Indra's departure, the flurry of activity ceased, and Indra's mother settled by the phone to wait for her daughter to reach and call her, even though this would take almost all day. An aunt who had decided to keep Shantha company on that difficult day saw her downcast face and helpfully (to her mind) said, "You know she'll be back in a few years. No need to be sad, Shantha. Start looking for a boy so she can get married as soon as she's back and settle down like all the other girls." But Shantha wasn't so sure.

•

Thirty thousand feet in the air, somewhere over the Indian Ocean, Indra was double checking that the dinner plate the stewardess had just handed her was vegetarian. Some fears would take a while to overcome. After dinner, she settled back in her uncomfortable seat, trying to get some sleep. Her ears had not hurt as much as her uncle had warned her, but there had been a few bumpy patches that no one had warned her about and that had made her stomach turn.

Thankfully, the plane landed for a stop-over soon. Sitting

upright in an alien airport in an alien country, Indra found herself feeling misty-eyed for the first time. Her cabin baggage—a small suitcase—already seemed to have a loose wheel. And suddenly there was a tear rolling down her cheek as she recalled the many arguments and discussions that had gone behind its purchase. Should it be hard or soft, a dark colour or a light one, how small or big? Indra once said about herself, "Behind my cool logic lies a very emotional person." And that would explain her sudden rush of nostalgia over cabin baggage! But she knew she could not indulge herself like that. With a quick swipe of her hand, she pushed the errant tear aside and sat up even straighter. Already, she had started coming to terms with a new sort of awareness of herself as someone with no one to depend on.

Back on the plane and another meal later, the interminably long flight eventually came to an end. Nervously, Indra collected all her papers—the I20 form, her passport and admission letter. Security measures weren't as fierce as they are today, and Indra was soon out of the airport and in America. It was the fall of 1980 and there at last was Indra in the country that would become her permanent home, but she didn't know that as she walked towards the bus terminal that would take her towards New Haven near Connecticut.

Climbing onto the bus, she realised it smelled different from the rusty tin ones in Chennai. Everything smelt different for that matter. Very... foreign. Indra was nervous but also felt a little thrill. She was abroad. At last.

Outside the window, everything seemed ten times larger than in India, be it the truck on the road or the road itself.

The sky was so much bluer and so clear. The trees literally reached up to the sky and what massive trunks they had! The only thing that was smaller in America were the people's eyes. Indians' eyes seemed larger and Indra's definitely were as she was taking it all in. Though she had had very little sleep over the last two days, she was wide awake now, observing, dissecting, examining America and comparing it to her country.

Reaching her campus at last, Indra spent a long time locating her room that was to be her home for the duration of her degree. Apart from her small suitcase, two large suitcases had to be transported to her room, and she had to do it alone with no father or uncle to give her a hand.

●

From the university brochure lying on the desk in her room, Indra learnt more about Yale. Reading the statistics, she was overwhelmed, wondering if she would be lost in a university of that scale and size, occupying no less than 600 acres. But she needn't have worried. Despite its sprawling campus and large number of students, Yale had also succeeded in creating a warm and friendly environment. It had divided the undergraduate population into twelve separate colleges with approximately 450 students each, thereby offering its students both the intimacy of a small college and the vast resources of a major research university. Besides, each college had its own dining hall, library, seminar rooms, recreation lounges, and other facilities.

When winter began to set in after a few months, Indra grew thankful for the ugly thermal underwear she had been forced to carry. But she was upset by her inability to prepare south Indian food in her room, where the slightest hint of smoke on the electric range would set off the sensitive fire alarm. All of these experiences Indra recorded in long letters that travelled around the world, taking several weeks or months to reach her home in Chennai, 88 GN Chetty Road, which had become a silent place.

Indra's younger brother was away for large parts of the day, attending school and playing with his friends. Shantha had doubled her prayer time while her father had taken to a more thorough reading of The Hindu. Temple going had also become a daily routine, far more intense and urgent than it had ever been.

The hours seemed to stretch. Where there used to be noise and laughter, now silence cast its listless arms over the whole family. Shantha's eyes kept stealing to the black phone she kept hoping would ring and bring with it the voice of one of her daughters.

Far away in Yale, life was so different. Indra had finally started on a path that would put her one day on Forbes Magazine's list of the most powerful women in the world.

Once I had gone to China,
Those whom I had not known before,
They put on my forehead a mark
Which said, "We know you."
The stranger's garb slipped from me
Revealing the inner man who is always the same...
A Chinese name I took, wore Chinese clothes
And I realised,
Wherever I find a friend, there I am born afresh.

— *Rabindranath Tagore* —

7

PREPARING FOR CORPORATE
AMERICA

Sitting in the common room of her dorm, Indra overheard many of her classmates animatedly talking about a sports team that never washed their uniforms after winning a match. "Superstition," said a lanky young man, responding to Indra's curious glance. He wore a baggy grey sweatshirt with YALE emblazoned across it. Superstition, did he say? In America?

"We're pretty superstitious about our sports in India too," replied Indra enthusiastically. "Cricket is this national obsession, and it is just the most beautiful sport!"

"Oh really?" said the boy wearing YALE across his chest.

"Oh yes, it's known as the gentleman's sport, you know.

Do you know much about cricket?"

"No, not really... there's a bat and ball and... yeah, that's about it."

"Oh it's a lot more than that. In cricket it's really all about the pitch. The moisture, the spin it gives the ball, and..."

Indra noticed the boy's eyes were glazing over. She trailed away, realizing he had no interest in what she was saying.

"Interesting..." he said in a bored voice. "But, you know, in baseball..."

And with that quick dismissal, the boy launched into a detailed description of the game of baseball. And unlike him, Indra listened with rapt attention.

Over the last few months, Indra had tried her best to expose herself to every aspect of American culture. She had realized that being happy in America did not mean teaching Americans about her culture but adapting to theirs. And she discovered that the easiest way to integrate herself and get on the same page as many of her co-students was through sports. "I didn't understand what they were talking about. I grew up with cricket," she said later.

She threw herself into life there and forged the bonds necessary to become a part of the culture rather than an outsider. A natural sportsperson, she especially learnt as much as possible about baseball, which is as dear to Americans as cricket is to Indians. She discovered that when it came to this sport, even some of the brightest minds studying at Yale became superstitious! Says Indra, about how she put her characteristic zeal to work: "Was I going to spend my life changing these people's ideas about cricket? Certainly not! So I decided to join the gang. I went to school on the New York Yankees. I studied every statistic. I became an expert on everything about the team. Unless one became part of the whole process, one could feel very left out."

In her motivation to learn about baseball, we can catch a glimpse of the Indra Nooyi who heads PepsiCo today. She was living her prescription for success, "Aim high and put your heart into it." If she wanted to just earn enough to settle down to a comfortable life, she may not have needed to know the intricacies of baseball. But when you want to get to the heart of things and be more than just average or 'good enough' then you have to overcome every single weakness of your heart. That is just what Indra was doing. How did she understand this at such a young age? Perhaps it was one of her mother's many confidence-building exercises in her childhood. Perhaps it was her innate sportsperson's spirit. But Indra understood early that success came through building effective teams, which one achieved through communication. And to communicate, she had to learn the language of her team. So Indra started learning the language of baseball as her first step towards building her team. As her other mantra states, "What's important is trying to be the best and working to get there. And that's how you fulfil your potential."

Indra's interest in baseball perhaps started as a way of bridging the cultural divide but she had a genuine interest in sports that has lasted until today. Much later in life, as CEO of PepsiCo, she is known to have spent hours studying videotapes of the final championship games that the basketball great, Michael Jordan played with the Chicago Bulls. She reviewed the tapes for lessons on teamwork!

Another tenet of Indra's is "never stop learning". Regardless of age or qualification, Indra's success in life can also be attributed to her open mind and learner's attitude. She believes that such learning should not be restricted to academic knowledge but be supplemented with "street smarts", by being aware of matters and issues in the real world. "Keep that natural curiosity," as she always says.

Clearly, for Indra, Yale was not just giving her a certificate or a degree in management but in life itself. She was learning and imbibing everything. One of the lessons she learnt stayed with her and helped her when she was called upon to head PepsiCo. She vividly describes this: "You know when I was in business school we went through two exercises. One was desert survival and one was arctic survival. What we had to do was pretend we were in a desert and were given ten things. Everybody in the group had to prioritize because you were only allowed to pick up five things and decide whether to stay or to walk and then they would videotape you. The professors would sit outside this one-way room and watch the group dynamics. How you bring others along with you was one of the biggest lessons Yale taught me, both desert survival and arctic survival."

In managing PepsiCo several years later, Indra says, "Interestingly, those principles of desert survival and arctic survival come back to me every time we sit down and talk about how to bring people along with us. How do you articulate that noble cause? How do you create a picture for them that where you want to take them is better than where they are today? It is not easy because each person's picture of the future or where they want to be is different from what you think the picture is going to be. The first step is really understanding the points of view of each of the people that are involved and then trying to craft the new or better vision for them and then taking them along with you. It is communication all the time. You might even argue that it is over-communication. Dick Detwiler handles communication for PepsiCo and I tell you we over-communicated to our people about the end state. After continuously talking about the end state in strong glowing terms, it is infectious because you get the opinion leaders on board with you. They carry the message to other people and pretty soon you have this movement that takes root."

Now what do you do with people that don't come along in the arctic survival game? Says Indra, "In every changed agenda there is always going to be a percentage of people, maybe 10%, who are not going to agree to the new agenda. They are the casualties of the change. If they have to go, they have to go. I think one of the challenges that we have is to take a call on those people after we have tried our best to bring them on the programme. We did lose people and I would say most of those people who have left would wish they hadn't left and stuck around. Many of them have come back to the company."

Recalling that the Graduate School of Management required all first-year students to take—and pass—a course in effective communications, she said in a 'Financial Times' interview that what she learnt in it "was invaluable for someone who came from a culture where communication wasn't perhaps the most important aspect of business, at least in my time."

From these descriptions, it is no wonder that Yale's MBA programme, the youngest in the Ivy League, has built a stellar reputation for its finance and strategy courses. In particular, Yale is known for its focus on non-profit and public management, with many graduates moving into such fields as mass transit, health-care management and telecommunications policy work.

Corporate recruiters in The Wall Street Journal/Harris Interactive survey have rated Yale MBA graduates as especially strong in strategic thinking, leadership potential, ability to work well in teams, communications and analytical and problem-solving skills. Yale also earned a good score for recruiters' satisfaction with the quality of graduates they have been able to hire in the past.

Surely much of these achievements have been because of its hugely qualified faculty. Indra's comments on one of her professors, the late Larry Isaacson who taught at Yale from 1976 to 1981, is evocative of the quality education she received there. "Larry was brilliant and demanding. He was full of questions, ideas, and delight in the accomplishments of his students. His approach to teaching was to give his students the skills they needed and then push them into the world to do good—and that is exactly what many of them have done. Larry's legacy is still alive in those he mentored at Yale SOM (School of Management)." Years later, Indra visited Yale to honour the memory of this professor by funding a portion of the new building in his memory.

Although on the one hand Indra was settling into her new life, making new friends and getting absorbed into the culture, on the financial front she was struggling to make ends meet. Though she received financial aid from Yale, she also had to take up a job. In typical Indra fashion—pushing herself to the limit—she worked as a receptionist, taking up the graveyard shift because it paid an additional 50 cents an hour. "My whole summer job was done in a sari because I had no money to buy clothes," says Indra, speaking of the hardships of that time but able to see the humour in it today.

She missed home though she was enjoying her time at Yale. Because she wasn't earning very well, she could not afford to call often and worked very hard to save just a little for a call. When she did call, the receiver would simply be passed from one member of the family to another, each one getting only enough time to say, "How are you, I am fine." She would put down the phone with the satisfaction of having heard everybody's voice, but no news was exchanged, no heart-to-heart conversation was possible.

Away from her family, the pressures she faced were many. "When I came to this country I had no safety net. If I failed, I failed. At the end of the month I would have $2 left over, and if I had $5 I thought I had died and gone to heaven. I had no money. I was dirt poor. At Yale I worked the receptionist counter from midnight to 5 am to make money. When you don't have a safety net, when you don't have money to buy clothes for interviews and you are going to a summer job in saris, all of a sudden life gives you a wakeup call and you realize that you have got to work extremely hard to make it happen in this country for you. Having grown up through all those hard knocks, through business school, through youth, you get a different perspective on life and you don't complain when you have to work hard now because if you are not working hard you think something is wrong. I have a different frame of reference when I approach my job. I know some of you are feeling tired just listening to me, but that is reality. That is how some of us work our way up to the top."

Even when she went for an interview at a prestigious business consulting firm, she wore a sari since she could not afford a business suit. But there is a story behind that. Indra says that when she went shopping for clothes to wear on that day "I did not look at skirts because I had never shown my legs before. I had only $50 with me. I picked up a $43 business suit from the local budget store and attended the job interview looking like the ultimate country bumpkin in my ill-fitting clothes. This had cost me $43. I had $7 left for shoes but could not get a decent pair for that sum. I thought, anyway my legs would be under the table so I could manage and wore garish orange snow boots. My appearance elicited a collective gasp from the people there. When I tearfully consulted my career development counsellor about my sartorial snafu, the latter advised me to wear a sari for my next interview, assuring me that 'if they can't accept you in a sari, it's their loss, not yours'." She wore a sari for her next interview with a very prestigious management consulting firm and clinched the job and learnt to say, "Never hide what makes you."

Indra learnt that while her interests and her understanding of the world could broaden to make her a truly global person, her inner core, her background, her upbringing were something she neither could nor wanted to change overnight, and this included her clothes and appearance. She attributes this value to her upbringing. And the lessons she was taught, both explicit and acquired, of being allowed to catch the thread of her dreams and weave it into a tapestry independently, regardless of whether that particular path or way of living or choice had been explored before. The idea also that family was of primary importance but with it as a support system, one should feel no doubt in chasing one's dreams.

And so at Yale, through academics as well as day-to-day life, Indra acquired a combination of intuitive business acumen, a burning ambition and the ability to make choices that foster one's innate strengths. Her graduation ceremony in 1980 was a true celebration for her as she had also received a job offer.

Today Indra is one of Yale's best known alumni and she serves on the board of trustees at the Yale Corporation, the governing board of Yale University. As she says, "I came to Yale as a young, intelligent immigrant. I left an educated, mature young executive, ready to face the challenges of Corporate America. Over the past 25 years, Yale has been my inspiration and support."

Walk with me/Four steps and three/Me and thee/Are heaven and earth/Seed am I/For thee to bloom/Come my mate and blend with me

— *Saptapadi* —

8

NEW BEGINNINGS

With the backing of an MBA from one of the world's finest universities, Indra set out on her path of becoming a respected businessperson. From Chennai to Connecticut...where to next? Many people believe we are defined by the cities in which we live, that the stories of our lives are inextricably entwined with the character of our cities.

Indra had started out as a conservative young girl, unsure of where her life was going, happy to spend time with her friends and play her guitar. This was her life when she was a student living in Chennai, surrounded by beaches and palm trees.

Connecticut had brought out a new aspect of her personality. She became an outgoing, bright young woman, independent and strong, more in control of her career and her destiny. As one of the earliest MBA graduates, Indra and her batch mates had a head start as candidates for jobs whose demand would only keep growing. Moreover, she had graduated from not just any school but an Ivy League university with an excellent reputation. She had good grades and stellar referrals from her professors, but when she thought of her last interview, her ears burned. In a bid to blend in with the other applicants dressed in skirts and jackets, Indra had splurged on an ill fitting pair of trousers and shirt that made her look rather clumsy. So conscious had she been of her clothes that she did not even remember the conversation that had taken place between her and her interviewers. In turn, those who had interviewed her, Indra felt, had been too shocked by her appearance to focus on the interview.

She had to clinch her next interview, for which she decided to go in a simple sari, on the advice of her career counsellor. She decided to just be herself. And it was a decision that would take her far. This call was from the Boston Consulting Group, a prestigious business consulting firm with offices in over thirty countries and its headquarters in Boston, Massachusetts. The man behind the BCG was Bruce Henderson, who went from being a Bible salesman to one of Time magazine's top ten newsmakers under the age of thirty.

Founded in 1963 by Henderson, the BCG initially started as the management and consulting division of the Boston

Safe Deposit and Trust Company. By 1965, Henderson felt a distinctive identity was needed. He pioneered "business strategy" as a special area of expertise for the BCG, and by 1974, it became an independent business unit.

Over the years, Henderson's reputation grew as did his company's. While on the one hand the BCG was steadily being recognized as one of the world's most illustrious business firms, on the other hand Henderson was writing books on business strategy that were being published in over twenty languages. As his client list grew, Henderson targeted the nation's best business schools. At some point he was said to have eclipsed McKinsey as the top recruiter at Harvard, aggressively wooing its best students with high salaries and the chance to make a difference in a cutting-edge firm. He encouraged the young minds he hired to come up with innovative ideas that were meant to dazzle hardened corporate veterans.

Henderson's story is the classic American dream and Indra was one of the many millions who dreamt it too. In her case, as in Henderson's, it came true. And it was in his company, and in his city, that it all started for Indra. In 1980 Indra joined the Boston Consulting Group. She knew it would be hard work, harder than for others, for two reasons—one, she was a woman, and two, she wasn't an American but an 'outsider'. "You know I will tell you one thing which some of you women may not like to hear, but accept it for whatever it is. The fact is that if you are a woman and especially a person of colour, there are two strikes against you. Immigrant, person of colour, and woman—three strikes against you. I can go on. If you want to reach the top of a company, it can only happen in the United States, but you have got to start off saying that you are going to work twice as hard as your counterparts. If you decide to get on a crusade and argue for equality and some kind of promotion, you could be on that crusade forever," said a determined Indra about her career and her personal strategy.

Indra spent six years directing international corporate strategy projects at the Boston Consulting Group. Her clients ranged from textile and consumer goods companies to retailers and speciality chemicals producers. She is the first to admit the price at which this success came. "This is just a personal point of view and I will tell you not just here, ever since I have been in work life I have always used that simple rule that whatever I did, I had to produce an output that was so much better than what somebody else did. So I would work extra hard at it. More hours, yes. More sacrifices and trade-offs, yes. That has been the journey. But the problem is, I don't know any other journey. This is the only journey I know. So I don't know what it is to have the cushy life and go home to watch the 6 o'clock news."

And with this job, for the next six years, Boston, along with Chennai and Connecticut, became yet another city to shape Indra's life. Her professional life. Indra Krishnamurthy, the brilliant businessperson. But what of Indra Krishnamurthy, the woman? She was now twenty-five years old, not yet too old but, in the eyes of her mother, no longer young. Shantha was proud of Indra's achievements, no doubt, but her greatest concern remained—marriage. Indra understood her mother's concerns and realized how within her context she appeared an almost unmarriageable commodity—a single girl living alone and working in America.

Even so, Indra had made it clear she did not wish to leave America any time soon. Her career was going well and she was certainly not about to give it all up to move back to Chennai and marry someone with lesser ambition and drive than her. Shantha was upset, but also knew her daughter's success lay in the land of opportunity. And then of course it was also the land of many good south Indian men who had settled there just like Indra! Shantha had also been seeing a lot of her friends' and neighbours' daughters getting married and leaving for the States. So she started badgering Indra about marriage almost daily.

Indra understood her mother's conflict, as she explained many years later: "I grew up with a mother who said 'I'll arrange a marriage for you at eighteen' but she also said that we could achieve anything we put our minds to and she encouraged us to dream of becoming prime minister or president. She made me learn Indian classical music because that's what good Indian girls did, but she also let me be in a rock band. 'You've got to be a good Indian woman first,' she said, 'but go ahead and dream'." And so Indra did not take her mother's constant refrain amiss. At the heart of it, she too was and still is a conservative Indian woman.

It so happened that while in the US, Indra met Rajkishan Nooyi, an engineer by profession. Raj Nooyi had done his bachelor's in engineering from the University of Mysore. He chose electronics and communication engineering at a time when this field was still emerging. All the bright young men of south India were west bound at that time, eager to get a degree from a foreign university that helped them realize their full potential. Like Indra, Raj too had done his Master's in Business Administration, from the University of Chicago after doing his MS in Industrial Engineering from the University of Texas, and had begun working with the Eaton Corporation in its manufacturing operations.

Later when Indra shot to fame as the CEO of PepsiCo, there was natural curiosity about her life. Her growing years were not tough to understand but all were stumped by her second name. It wasn't just the west—the name is unfamiliar to Indians too. Actually Nooyi wasn't just the last name of her husband but also of the town in a long list of others to shape Indra's destiny. Raj's family hails from a village in Karnataka called Gurupur where Nooyi is a common and well-known name. The district in which the village lies is also known for other celebrities, including Aishwarya Rai, former Miss World and reigning Bollywood actor.

The Nooyi family is well known in Gurupur. Raj's uncle, Srinivasa Rao, is an advocate. Mrs Sooryanarayan, Raj's mother, is very religious, with an affinity for Guruvayur, the Krishna temple in Kerala, and the Subramanyam Temple near Mangalore. In her, Indra's mother found a kindred spirit.

In 1983 Indra and Raj were married. The same year, Raj moved from the Eaton Corporation to Hewlett Packard as a manager. Indra too was being promoted—to a mother! Their baby was due the following year. All of Shantha's dreams for her daughter had come true. But for Indra, there were still miles to go...

As a role model to millions of young girls around the world, Indra has spoken openly not just about her path to professional success but her personal successes as well. She said, "You have to pick the right husband. I picked the right husband. Raj is a great guy and he has been a great support and I do not know where I would have been without him. I would say that without a doubt. He has been more than a husband. He has been a sounding board or friend."

"I remember my mother's prayers and they have always followed me.
They have clung to me all my life."

— *Abraham Lincoln* —

9

BALANCING WORK AND FAMILY

Home now was more than just a place to sleep at night.
Along with Raj, Indra built a home that was a haven,
an escape from their busy schedules. Raj never stood in the
way of Indra's ambitions, and he too travelled five days a
week for work. And so their time together at home was all
the more special, a sanctuary with Carnatic music constantly
playing in the background—and a Karaoke machine of course!

The family of two grew with the birth of their first
child, Preetha. Suddenly, Indra's mother's worries and concerns
that would once amuse Indra started to make perfect sense.
Her sister Chandrika and her brother Narayanan were also

married by then and settled in America. The sisters often spoke of finally understanding what it must have been like for Shantha to be responsible for two daughters.

Shantha of course considered herself tremendously lucky. All her children were married and settled. True her daughters had not married strictly within the community but she was very proud to say both her sons-in-law were worth their weight in gold. They fostered her daughters' ambitions and were a great support to them. Chandrika had married a Punjabi, Indra a Mangalorean, and her son Narayanan had married a Tamil Brahmin. Shantha brought all this diversity within one room—her pooja room!

●

Indra was gradually growing more aware of the importance of family. But unlike many other women of her time, this was not at the cost of her career. Raj had just moved to the IT giant, Hewlett Packard. And there was no way Indra was going to sacrifice moving up the ranks in her career after Preetha's birth. Her mother's lessons came to her rescue at a time when she was torn between home and work. She realized that what she had always seen as her mother's conflict—her focus on getting her daughters married but also doing well professionally—was in fact the ultimate lesson in balance. In the role of a mother now, Indra performed all of her duties but remained the strategist at heart. She realized her challenge lay in being able to balance work and home.

To begin with, Indra left her job at the Boston Consulting Group after six successful years. Her work there had given her the sound strategic background she needed and enabled her to join the telecommunications company Motorola as Vice President and Director of Corporate Strategy and Planning.

In 1986 when Indra joined Motorola, the company had just developed a six sigma quality process that soon became the global quality standard. It was during Indra's tenure that Motorola introduced the world to the first pager which transformed communication and became the precursor to the mobile phone revolution. Although the company became best known for this, Indra's equally critical work was as business development executive for the company's automotive and industrial electronic group.

Four years later, in 1990, she moved to ASEA Brown Boveri, a $6 billion Swiss-Swedish automation and power company where she spent four years as Vice President, Corporate Strategy and Planning. She was part of the top management team as the head of strategy, responsible for the company's US business as well as its worldwide industrial businesses, generating about one-third of ABB's $30 billion of global sales. At the time Indra entered the company it was bringing about many changes and expanding to new horizons and territories. Indra was part of this exciting process, in a position where her contribution was significant.

Her skill in helping ABB find its direction in North America came to the attention of Jack Welch, then Chairman and CEO of General Electric. He offered her a job in 1994, but so did PepsiCo Chief Executive Officer, Wayne Calloway. As she told a writer for Business Week, the two men knew one another, but Calloway made a much more appealing pitch.

He told her, Indra recalled, "Welch is the best CEO I know...
But I have a need for someone like you, and I would make
PepsiCo a special place for you."

Indra chose the soft drink maker and became its chief
strategist. It was a move that was to change her life. PepsiCo
was and continues to be one of the world's most respected
and profitable multinationals and was to give Indra's career
precisely the fillip she—and her mother!—had been praying
for.

But Indra was aware that the promotion would come
at a cost. Preetha was growing up and needed more attention.
Indra summarizes it with these words: "You can walk away
from the fact that you're a corporate executive, but you can't
walk away from the fact that you are a mom. In terms of
being a mother and a corporate executive, the role of mom
comes first."

Indra and Raj knew their careers would not allow them
to give her the same amount of time their mothers had given
them. And they were not keen on having their children raised
entirely by baby sitters. So she and Raj began wooing their
relatives. As Indra explains, "Both of us, Raj and I, did not
want to leave our child with nannies or babysitters. We felt
somebody from the family would be good. So we went that
extra mile to keep the extended family happy, buying them
gifts, keeping in touch with as many as possible and taking
their help when required."

Raj's mother often pitched in, and Shantha and
Krishnamurthy would visit their children as well. But with
both of Indra's siblings living in New York, there was a constant
tug of war for Shantha's time, with all her children wanting

to spend time with her and have her living with them.

For Indra's children, Shantha was the only source of tradition and traditional values that Indra and her siblings had been raised with. As she explains, "Now my mother lives with me, and my kids see her praying, so they too sit down and pray with her. Two days ago when my little daughter was feeling sick, she went and lay on my mother's lap. She chanted hymns and caressed her; after a while my daughter said she felt much better."

That's today—but all those years ago Indra often worried about her daughter not knowing what it meant to come from a middle class background. She strongly believed it was her background that had given her and her siblings a certain balance in their lives. She knew what it was to not have new clothes every year and to ration two buckets of water through the day. It was these things that, later in life, helped Indra become a smart money manager as well as strategize for her companies. On the one hand her maternal instinct made her want to protect her daughter from life's hardships but she also knew there were important lessons she had learned from her struggles, both in conservative Chennai and as an Indian woman trying to succeed in America's cut-throat corporate world.

Through all of this, she continued to remain uncompromising on some basic things. For example, Indra never tasted meat or alcohol, and although she may have been seen as an anomaly at first, today she says, "Now when we go out, even my chairman will tell everybody to make sure there's vegetarian food for Indra." And this was precisely the kind of steadfast grounding she wanted her children to have as well.

In India, life seemed to begin and end with religious faith, something that had been ingrained in Indra from a young age. Their home in the US therefore had a pooja room, like her home in Chennai, but it was visits from Indra's mother and mother-in-law that she most valued. It was these two women who gave her daughter a true sense of confidence and courage in the Almighty. Respect towards food, respect for elders, care for the extended family and rituals were some of the values that Indra fervently wished her daughter to imbibe. She knew that it was the seemingly small things— the dot of sacred ash *(vibhuti)* on the forehead, the red thread twisted around the wrist—that held the family to its roots.

Indra values religion in her life, and her daughter's life. "It certainly makes me calm," she says. "There are times when the stress is so incredible between office and home, trying to be a wife, mother, daughter-in-law and corporate executive. Then you close your eyes and think about a temple like Tirupati, and suddenly you feel, 'Hey, I can take on the world.' Hinduism floats around you, and makes you feel somehow invincible."

If religion is one pillar, what is the other? The answer comes pat: "My family. If all else fails, I call my mother in India when she's there and wake her up in the middle of the night and she listens to me. And she probably promises god a visit to Tirupati!"

Brothers and sisters are as close as hands and feet.

— *Vietnamese proverb* —

10

SIBLINGS WITHOUT RIVALRY

"He's smarter than both of us," Indra says with a smile whenever she is asked about her brother Narayanan. Yes, Indra Nooyi is the Krishnamurthy sibling who is a celebrity. But in her eyes, her siblings were the ones deserving of the attention. Chandrika and Narayanan may have fewer mentions in newspaper articles than their sister, but the lessons of life that had brought Indra this success were the same that enabled her siblings to make their mark in the corporate world too.

By the nineties, it had become quite commonplace for Indians to migrate to America. Indra, Chandrika and

Narayanan were three of many, but three who made a true mark. The three Krishnamurthys who were simply the kids next door in T Nagar eventually took over their respective professional domains on international shores. All three siblings received an American education and have made America their new home, each scaling the heights of success.

After fifteen years of being a consultant, in 1992, Indra's elder sister Chandrika Tandon founded an advisory and investment firm that advises Fortune 500 companies on streamlining and re-engineering their operations. She has been described as "the re-engineering master who has spearheaded the streamlining of several banks in recent years." Her New York-based Tandon Capital Associates, whose speciality is making banks more efficient and profitable, has in the last few years been responsible for several banks saving more than $680 million in expenditure. So effective are the company's solutions, it has acquired the nickname 'The Tandonistas'!

Prior to this, Chandrika worked for Citibank in Beirut, in currency trading, operations and branch management. Thereafter, she spent eleven years at McKinsey & Company, five of them as a partner. Over the years, she has worked with the senior management of some of the most prominent banking, insurance and securities companies in the world.

Chandrika has kept her Indian roots well watered. She is a contributor to many philanthropic causes and has a deep interest in supporting the arts and the livelihood of underprivileged women. She is a board member and trustee of the American India Foundation, chairing the initiative to create sustainable livelihoods among the rural and urban poor in India. She has also founded the League of Artisans programme that aims to create a unifying platform to build sustainable business enterprises in the craft sector. She is on the Board of the Indo American Arts Council, an organization devoted to promoting awareness of India-influenced art forms in the US. She is executive-in-residence at the Stern School of Business at New York University, and founder and chairman of the League of Artisans.

Ranjan Tandon, her husband, heads Libra Investors, a major hedge fund, and they have a daughter, Lita, who has, like Indra, gone on to study at Yale.

In all of these professional achievements, however, Chandrika has not forgotten her spiritual side, the rituals and prayers she learned as a child from her mother. Chandrika and her husband both make it a point to start their day with meditation and *pranayam,* the ancient technique of breathing. Says Chandrika, "[Ranjan] feels it makes him a much better investor, because of the clarity it gives him... It's really about a set of processes which help you. It's almost as if you blow out the stress. The techniques and processes like meditation, *pranayam* and yoga are exercises to help the inner polishing."

Both Chandrika and Indra have been at the forefront of the movement that has today made spirituality and meditation a part of the corporate world. Chandrika says, "It's an exciting time and I think all of us are a part of that—that to me is a very powerful form of spirituality. This is about the whole transformation of the consciousness of one from the inside, and you use many, many approaches to change that."

Her spiritual growth has helped foster a more

compassionate work culture for Chandrika as well: "Knowing what I know now, I would have thought of a lot of my business decisions differently ten years ago."

Today yoga, meditation and prayer are being seen as valid management methodologies and gaining acceptance in the western world as much as in India. Even in Chandrika's line of work, which involves taking tough decisions and aggressive stands on a daily basis, the gentle art of breathing right fits right in. Chandrika does not find her work and spirituality to be at loggerheads at all. "You begin to take a more integrated, more holistic, more compassionate view of things, and I don't think the two are in conflict at all. You have to really not look just at company profits, but you really start to look at the issues of people, you start to look at issues of giving back, of not destroying the environment."

When her daughter Lita, who is a sophomore at Yale University, turned eighteen, her parents' gift to her was an Art of Living meditation course. Chandrika explains, "We teach children about reading, writing and arithmetic, but we don't teach them how to manage stress and how to calm themselves. They have a more difficult time than our generation did."

What about the sibling both sisters consider the smartest one? Younger than both his sisters by approximately a dozen years, Narayanan Krishnamurthy is making a name for himself on Wall Street as an investment adviser and portfolio manager. He followed his sister Indra's footsteps in choosing Yale as his alma mater and went to study there at seventeen. He then went on to get accepted into the Massachusetts Institute of Technology's renowned Sloane School of Management.

Looking back on the sacrifices their mother Shantha made, her burning ambition for her children, she perhaps knew what the world didn't—that she was raising three children who would, in many ways, transform the world, making a difference to people's lives, contributing to the wealth of this earth.

If your actions inspire others to dream more
learn more, do more
and
become more
you are a leader
— *John Quincy Adams* —

11

PEPSICO

It was in 1994, still relatively young at forty-four, that Indra joined PepsiCo as Senior Vice President, Corporate Strategy and Development, working directly with CEO, Roger Enrico. The world thought she had broken the glass ceiling. Little did they realize this was just the beginning. Indra's ambition was as usual far ahead of the world's expectations of her.

When she moved from ABB to PepsiCo, she did more than just change jobs. She made the decision that would change her and her family's life forever. Indra's family too had changed. She now had two daughters, Preetha and who needed even more of Indra's time and attention. Both personally and professionally, Indra had entered her most productive and creative phase.

It was a time when Indra became comfortable in her role as corporate head honcho on the one hand and mom of two on the other. In fact, she stopped seeing them as two separate functions. As she said in an interview with Business India in 2001, "I love my family, but PepsiCo's also my child. So really I don't look upon it as a chore. In fact, I find work very therapeutic."

Indra knew that getting to that position was one thing; staying there was another matter altogether. "If you want to reach the top of a company, I agree that it can only happen in the United States, but you have to start off saying that you have got to work twice as hard as your [male] counterparts." And that's exactly what she did.

When she joined the company, there were three primary businesses. PepsiCo was most well known for its soft drinks, which included both bottled drinks as well as concentrates. The second business was of salted snacks, which included the well-known Frito Lay. And then there were the restaurants—Pizza Hut, Kentucky Fried Chicken (KFC), Taco Bell and a large number of casual dining chains. Until 1994, each of these three businesses was performing well and the company enjoyed a stellar reputation.

In an interview with 'The Economic Times', Indra talks about the corporate turnaround that enabled her to show what she was truly capable of.

The restaurant arm of PepsiCo's business was, until 1994, a thriving business. The company had acquired many of the brands about a decade earlier and invested billions of dollars into them. Within two months of Indra joining, things started to change. "Around 1994-95, the restaurant business started softening, and softening in a dangerous way. We didn't like the business trend. Roger Enrico came in back from a sabbatical, and he became head of the restaurant sector which at that time didn't have anyone. So Wayne Calloway, then CEO, appointed Roger as the head of the restaurant sector and I was his chief of staff having just joined the company. So in '94, Roger and I undertook a sweeping re-look at the restaurant business. We didn't take any action on the restaurant business; we were trying to understand as to what was going on with the business—that it had been such a high flying one, and all of a sudden the performance fell. It was really falling. And the wonderful thing is both Roger and I didn't know the restaurant business. We had to learn it from scratch. We had no biases, we had no hidden agendas, we didn't have any baggage we were carrying. We just went and worked our way up and down the restaurants of every city," says Nooyi, recollecting those days.

Those were intense days of hard work. Together, Indra and Roger would just hop on a plane and travel all around the US, visiting their own as well as competitors' restaurants from morning till evening. They didn't miss a thing: "Front of the house, back of the house, and what other people said… everything. We checked quality, hygiene, everything. We tried to understand the economics of the restaurant business… Then we tried to understand the saturation of restaurants. We tried to understand what has changed in this business between 1987, '88, '89 and till 1994 that all of a sudden traffic is down, profitability is down. Is it the whole industry's profit fall or is it the way we run the restaurants?"

The hard work paid off and the pair soon came up with a theory to explain the sudden downturn in their restaurants' earnings. "What has happened to the restaurant business is that the profitability has fallen the way it has, worse than what it was in the late '80s when it was such a high flyer... Doing this sort of a bottom-up analysis, with no biases, yielded some fascinating results. This to me is perhaps the best piece of work we did in a long time, because what it showed was the industry had saturated and too many quick service restaurants had been built, because if you didn't build the next quick service restaurant, somebody else built it."

Indra described the restaurant business at the time as a prisoner's dilemma, a 'damned if you do, damned if you don't' situation. "If you built it, you cannibalize your own concept, but if you didn't build it, somebody else is going to cannibalize that concept. So you were in this terrible vicious cycle."

Together Indra and Enrico re-inspected PepsiCo's entire restaurant policy from top to bottom. The strictly objective approach led to some key learning. The two realized that a restaurant wasn't a fully profitable asset unless it was being utilized to the maximum. "If you look at Pizza Hut, it only had lunch and dinner and didn't have a breakfast. And if you look at KFC... we were not catering to the twenty four-hour meal cycle."

The next realization was that the profit of a restaurant was closely tied to its real estate, which is in many ways "the key driver of the restaurant's performance." This driver, in the mid-nineties was getting scarce. The situation was slightly complex. On paper, PepsiCo owned all its capital, since, in most cases, they owned the real estate. "But," explains Indra, "we had many, many tens of thousands of restaurants. We didn't own all of them. We owned about, at that time, 50-60% of the restaurants, the rest were franchised."

The decision that came next was the logical outcome. "The first thing we said was, let's take our restaurants and re-franchise them. Because, if you walk into Pizza Hut and you don't like the interaction, you do not come back. So, the quality of the labour became critical. We are not a big labour management company, and based on our calculations, PepsiCo would have needed half a million people just in the restaurant business."

This mind boggling figure turns even more so when Nooyi adds, "If you think about shifts, [there were] three shifts. And multiply this by tens of thousands [of people]. And the attrition rate! It's terrible," says Nooyi. "It is very hard to get good people and by the time you do the background check on them and get them in, it is just impossible. So, we looked at this and said, my God, this is not the PepsiCo kind of business at all. And those who love the restaurant business, have restaurants in their blood, want to have a steady labour pool—they're the people that should own the restaurant. So we started to re-franchise huge chunks of the business. We started selling off to franchisees, independent people, either existing franchisees or new people. That is the first step we took in 1995-96."

A year later, in 1996, Indra's strategic side kicked in again when she and Enrico began to question their own decision. Indra explains, "In 1996, we said that re-franchising is good, but does this business really belong to us? What would happen is, we would bring high-flying MBAs into the company and rotate them through senior jobs very quickly. What we realized was for them to grow in PepsiCo, you have to put them in the restaurant business. But when you put them in as a District Manager-Restaurants, they knew nothing about restaurants. You really needed a restaurant person to run restaurants."

PepsiCo was essentially a packaged foods company, and Indra along with her colleagues realized that they were imposing a packaged foods culture on the restaurant business. No wonder it was failing. "What we were doing was, in fact, burdening the restaurant business with the packaged foods culture. So, we realized what we had to do, at that point, was to un-tether the restaurant business from the packaged foods business. So, we really unburdened the restaurant business rather than unburden PepsiCo because we were destroying the restaurant business by meshing it within the packaged foods culture."

They then took the difficult decision of de-merging the restaurants. From the outside, this seemed like a ridiculous solution. It meant cutting down the company's assets from $30 billion to $20 billion in one move. But the risk paid off.

"We spun it off to its shareholders and it started doing exceedingly well. I was at YUMI Restaurants two weeks ago, and just the whole culture of the place is different—the way they talk, the way they act, the way they care for their customers. It is not that we don't care for customers, they deal with this at a very different level and there has been a huge success doing so."

Nooyi agrees the decision was bold. She overcame the traditional multinational approach of merely building a business in size and scale. Indra's strategic side told her the smarter decision was to disengage from a line of business that was suffering and causing the parent company to suffer as well. "And getting rid of friends, because everybody in the restaurant business grew up in PepsiCo. We grew that business. Wayne Calloway loved the business. John Kendall loved the restaurant business. So it was the most painful decision we made. We had no vested emotion in that business. And, we started up saying it is easier to sell a business or kill it than it is to grow a business, so let's try our best to grow what we have got. Because very few people have businesses they can grow. We had terrific brands, so we started off by saying we really want to grow this business, not spin it off."

The million dollar question is, how did she manage to pull it off? PepsiCo is a large, multi-layered corporation, and the decision couldn't have been Indra's alone. Indra would have needed the consensus of the entire board and as often happens, the better the idea, the tougher it is to convince people. So how did Indra manage to convince everybody, particularly when it targeted a company's carefully built assets over many years and spelt a complete change of profile? What happened when she stood up to make that presentation to the board?

The man who removes a mountain begins by carrying away small stones

— *Chinese proverb* —

12

THE MASTER STRATEGIST

I n hindsight, the decision to re-franchise was precisely what PepsiCo needed to salvage its flagging profit margin and reputation. But sitting in an empty conference room with Roger Enrico, a hush hanging above their heads save for the low drone of the air conditioner, the two had a lot on their minds.

"This is really drastic," said Enrico.

"Yup."

"They're not going to take this very well."

"Nope."

"Are we going to be able to pull this off?"

Indra didn't bother with the monosyllabic response this time and simply shrugged, the woven shawl draped on her right shoulder moving up, then down. Enrico looked at the woman sitting before him, short in stature, youthful in appearance, but with an intensely steely look in her eye.

"You're completely sure about this, aren't you?"

"Yup."

And that's all she needed to say. Enrico was convinced too; he was just looking for a final confirmation, and Indra's firm resolve had given it to him.

In a couple of hours, the PepsiCo board of directors would file into that very conference room to attend their presentation on how to rescue PepsiCo's failing restaurant business. They knew what the board wanted to hear-more investments, higher employment, expansion, growth, renewal... But what they were going to say was precisely the opposite.

For the first time that day, Indra broke her introspective silence.

"Roger, you know and I know re-franchising is the way to go. It's the only way to go. We're right and we know it and that's all we have to say. The rest is up to them. So let's stop over-thinking it and just do it. Okay?"

It was Enrico's turn to be monosyllabic.

"Okay."

"Okay."

A few hours later, the two were standing before the board,

with Indra giving her first critical presentation as Vice President of the company.

She says, "We did it in a very interesting way. The first step was just showing them the strategic analysis of a restaurant business. We didn't tell them that we want to spin it off. We said that these are the economics of the restaurant industry. This is what is happening. These are the four options we have. What do you think should be the option we should go for? We didn't put it out then. We said these are the options and we would like to come back to you with the consequences of pursuing two of the four options that we would like to push some more. The board said yes, we should push it some more. So when we pushed through the analysis on the two options we sort of zeroed in on, it was crystal clear that the spin off was the best option. So, it was a very deliberate, iterative process. It was not one of those things where we said, just close it off. "

It is in situations like this that one gets to see Nooyi's strategic abilities. She made her board a part of the decision instead of confronting them with the radical idea. "Our board was involved. Every step of it and, I must say, the board contributed hugely to the discussion and it was an excellent discussion." She turned her decision into a discussion, almost letting the board feel that it was their own decision!

But Indra's master plan wasn't complete. She still had one trick up her sleeve. Although her proposal to re-franchise had been accepted, she too was not happy about having cut her company's assets by a third. In a strategic masterstroke, she replenished their assets by attempting—and succeeding—at acquiring a brand that would add value to PepsiCo's repertoire. Indra says, "Right after that, we bought Tropicana. And Tropicana was a very important acquisition because up to that time, PepsiCo's brands in the beverage sector only became relevant after 10 o'clock in the morning. So from 5 am to 10 am, our brands were almost not relevant. We thought that as a very important part of the day that we had to capture. We could have built a brand ourselves, but the point is when you have a brand like Tropicana, which was good for breakfast and good for you, we decided to buy it. It was a part of Seagram at that time. They were following two tracks, IPO or sale. So we bid [for the company] and bought it in 1997."

An important point to note here is that Indra's interest in Tropicana wasn't simply from a strategic or financial point of view, although that was a large part of it. She also believed PepsiCo needed to start focusing on more products that were genuinely good for people—fresh juice being a clear example—rather than products that people simply enjoyed—like the salted snacks they sold. When years later Indra would become CEO, she would come to draw a clear distinction between these products that she dubbed 'fun for you' products (the salted snacks and cola drinks the company was best known for at the time) and those she called 'better for you' and 'good for you'. These were the two product categories Indra would later focus on developing as CEO, and the Tropicana acquisition was her first step in that direction.

A personal fan of Tropicana's orange juice, Nooyi understood before others Tropicana's brand potential, both to increase PepsiCo's earnings as well as to enhance the company's developing portfolio of convenience and 'functional' foods and drinks. Furthermore, Indra had also predicted, very early on, the future slowdown in the popularity of aerated soft drinks in markets worldwide. "When other PepsiCo executives continued to question the $3.3 billion acquisition at a final meeting, Roger and I just told them, 'We are going to do it'."

At the time of the acquisition, PepsiCo's foremost competitor was Coca-Cola. Speaking of this, Indra said, "When we were buying Tropicana, the Coca-Cola company's stock price was almost $80 and much more than twice our stock price. They were the darling. So, we went to school on the Coca-Cola company, trying to find out what they do right, what they don't do right, what works, what doesn't."

The rivalry between Pepsi, the flagship product of Indra Nooyi's company, and its Atlanta, Georgia-based competitor, Coca-Cola, is one of corporate America's longest-running marketing battles. In the United States alone, the soft drink industry is a $60 billion one, with the average American consuming a staggering fifty-three gallons of carbonated soft drinks every year.

The battle between Coke and Pepsi dates almost as far back as each company's history. Both emerged as key players in the early decades of the twentieth century when soft drinks first appeared on the market in the United States. In the 1920s, Coca-Cola began moving aggressively into overseas markets and even opened bottling plants near places where US service personnel were stationed during World War II. Pepsi only moved into international territory in the 1950s but scored a major coup in 1972 when it inked a deal with the Soviet Union. With this deal, Pepsi became the first

Western product ever sold to Soviet consumers.

The battle for market share heated up after 1975 when both companies stepped up their already lavishly financed marketing campaigns to win new customers. Pepsi's standard cola products had a slightly sweeter taste, which prompted one of the biggest corporate-strategy blunders in US business history: in 1985, to counter Pepsi's sweeter taste, Coca-Cola launched "New Coke," which had a slightly sweeter formulation. Coke consumers were outraged. The old formula was still available under the name "Coca-Cola Classic" but the New Coke idea was quickly shelved. This incident is often a part of business-school curricula in the United States and elsewhere, along with many other aspects of what is known as "the cola wars".

Coke is the leader in market share for carbonated colas but soft drinks remain its core business. Pepsi, on the other hand, began acquiring other businesses in 1965 when it bought the Texas-based Frito-Lay company, and acquired a larger stake in the food industry.

One of the key lessons from the Coke study was the importance of spinning off labour-intensive businesses that require the kind of day-to-day focus a franchise company cannot afford. Coke, for instance, had spun off its bottling operation—a labour-intensive business—and this had given them several advantages. Ten years after Coke had done it, PepsiCo too spun off its bottling business, but rectifying all of Coke's errors. Instead of simply spinning off, they went in for an IPO (Initial Public Offer) for the bottling business.

While the franchise company had to focus on the brands, it needed big investments, unlike the PepsiCo packaged foods brand, Frito Lay. One could argue, after all, that the old Frito Lay was an operating entity. Why was this business different? Indra explains, "Unlike Frito Lay where distribution is everything, in the beverage business [both] a franchise company and the distribution company are important. So, it is critical for us that we look at these as two entities. Again, we realized our strength is in franchise business. But you need a very operative culture to run a distribution business, which is precisely why Coke spun off its bottling units."

The decisions PepsiCo was taking had by now cost it a total of $17 billion. Indra the strategist did not look at what had gone. She looked at what she had. "Now, I had Tropicana," she says explaining her optimistic stance, though she had gone from $30 million to $13 million. But she wasn't worried. There were still more tricks up her sleeve.

In the mid-1990s, Enrico asked Indra to develop a strategy that would make PepsiCo the "defining corporation for the 21st century", more like GE. This was the kind of meaty strategic challenge that was Indra's forte. She began work on drawing up various scenarios of what that might look like via path A, B or C. Together, Enrico and Indra picked a path, and part of that path was the acquisition of the Quaker Oats brand. Explains Indra, "Tropicana brought in a little over $3 billion. And then Quaker Oats brought in $7 billion. So, it was there. We have written a case study on it and it has all the decision making and how we went through it, but I think it was an incredible financial transformation, because return on invested capital went from 15% to 25%. Cash flow on $30 billion of revenue was like a billion something and on $20 billion of revenue—$10 billon less—

it was over $3 billion. So it was a transformation." When asked about her level of involvement in these game-changing decisions, Indra modestly says, "This was not an individual activity at all."

"Buying of the Quaker Oats company was very critical. One, for the Gatorade business. It was an area that we were not very successful in, the isotonic business, and Gatorade had an 80% share of the isotonic business. So we felt that was a very critical acquisition to make. They created the isotonic category. But the other reason we bought Quaker Oats, which very few people really understand, is because it was again similar to the Tropicana acquisition. If you look at Frito Lay, if you want to make a healthy product, you could not use any other Frito products, brands. To call them Frito Bar or the Lays Bar or Ruffles Bar and expect to use it for breakfast would be crazy. They just did not have the right association. We needed another brand. So we knew we needed a nutrition-credential backed brand to launch a whole range of good food products. So the brand Quaker, when we did all our brand studies, was clearly on the top."

During the complex negotiations, Indra demanded a limit on the stock price of no more than $105 per share for Quaker shareholders. Steven Baronoff, co-head of mergers at Merrill Lynch, which represented PepsiCo, told the 'Contra Costra Times' in December 2000, "Throughout the whole process, she was disciplined and held very firm." So in about five years' time, Indra had been the chief dealmaker for two of PepsiCo's most important acquisitions—she put together the $3.3 billion dollar deal for the purchase of the Tropicana orange juice brand in 1998, and two years later was part of the team that secured Quaker Oats for $14 billion. That became one of the biggest food deals in corporate history and added a huge range of cereals and snack food products to the PepsiCo empire. She also helped acquire the beverage maker SoBe for $337 million, and her deal beat the one submitted by Coca-Cola.

Laying out just the facts in this way can be misleading. From the outside, it appears as if Indra could do no wrong, that she was supremely self-confident and sure of each step as she took it. In reality, however, perfect self-confidence is impossible, and Indra too was feeling the stress. After a tough session with the Quaker Oats executives, she confesses to having flown to Pittsburgh to pray at a shrine of her family's deity. Amidst all of the tough business decisions, Indra was also focused on keeping her team well, happy and efficient. She would often watch championship game replays of the Chicago Bulls to study teamwork concepts, for example, and admitted to Forbes magazine that she strategizes 24/7. "I wake up in the middle of the night," she told the magazine, "and write different versions of PepsiCo on a sheet of paper."

Her quick decision making ability and her ability to stick to the job until it was accomplished drew this comment from the then chief of PepsiCo, Roger Enrico: "If she gets an idea, she goes after it. There's no stopping her."

For her impressive deal making talents, Nooyi was promoted to the position of Chief Financial Officer at PepsiCo in February 2000. It made her the highest-ranking Indian-born woman among the ranks of corporate America. Indra proved her worth when she finished that financial year with four continuous quarters of uninterrupted growth in revenues, profits and returns on capital. By December 2000, the company's stock price was up 40% from the previous year.

Within a year of being named CFO, in 2001 Indra was also made President of the company by PepsiCo CEO Roger Enrico. Following the Quaker Oats acquisition, Enrico announced, "Indra's contributions to PepsiCo have been enormous and she will make a great President. In addition to her new role as President and CFO, Indra will also be nominated for election to the Pepsi board. She is a terrific addition to our world-class board and her perspective will be invaluable."

Indra was thirty-nine when she joined PepsiCo. By her forty-fifth birthday, she had been involved in every major strategic decision of the company, including the move to spin off PepsiCo's fast food chain in 1997, Tropicana's acquisition in 1998 and the acquisition of Quaker Oats in 2001. The applause for these achievements echoed around the world. But Indra, as usual, had more tricks up her sleeve....

Learning brings humility, humility develops capability, capability brings wealth and wealth and righteousness bring happiness.

— *Subhashita* —

13

PERFORMANCE WITH PURPOSE

It was about 10 pm and the newly appointed President of PepsiCo was just getting home after a hard day. She had recently managed the acquisition of Quaker Oats, for which she had been promoted to President, but the acquisition wasn't going as smoothly as she'd have liked. Merging the Gatorade and Tropicana sales forces had resulted in a botched sales promotion, and a key Quaker Oats executive had resigned. Supermarket sales of Gatorade, Quaker's crown jewel, were up by only 7% in the last quarter of 2001 compared to the 15% pace set by its market peers.

Needless to say, Indra had a lot on her mind as she

parked her car in their three-car garage. Her husband Rajkishan's car was already there. She smiled, glad he was home. Because amidst all the work tension, she was excited to share the news of her promotion with her entire family. Her parents too were staying with her for a few weeks and she was delighted she'd be able to break the news to them in person rather than on the telephone.

As she shut the door behind her, she heard her mother call out from the kitchen, "Indra, is that you?"

"Yes, Mom," she called out. She was bursting to give her the news.

Placing her briefcase on the table, Indra all but sprinted to the kitchen.

"Hey, Mom!"

Entering the kitchen, she realized she was speaking to her mother's back. Shantha was busy stirring a stew at the electric gas range.

"Mom! I have some important news!"

"Leave that important news, just go buy some milk first," Shantha said over her shoulder.

Indra's smile quickly turned into a frown.

"Raj is home, why don't you ask him to buy the milk?"

"He is tired," pat came the reply.

Indra began to fume. Typical mother-can't disturb the son-in-law! She whirled around and left the house to buy the milk, slamming the door shut behind her. Shantha barely noticed and continued stirring her stew.

After a few minutes, Indra came back carrying two cartons

of milk which she slammed down on the kitchen table.

"Tell me, why do I have to buy the milk and not somebody else?"

For the first time, Shantha seemed to notice her daughter's rage. She turned around calmly and said in an even tone, "Look, when you pull into the garage, leave the crown there. Don't walk in with it, because you are first a wife and a mother. And if the family needs milk, you go get the milk. That is your primary role in life. Everything else you got because I pray for four to five hours a day."

Recalling this incident some years later, Indra laughingly said, "That is the only thing she tells me, 'What did you accomplish? You sit in a meeting on a chair all the time, and I pray for 4-5 hours!'" Perhaps Indra's own contribution to her success has not been as small as Shantha claims, but Indra does credit her mother with much of what she has got in life. And she especially remembers the powerful lesson she learnt in the kitchen that night.

●

With her mother's wisdom and the humility she had taught her, Indra went on to achieve great success at PepsiCo. And as she moved up the ranks, so did long-time colleague Steven S. Reinemund, who advanced to the position of Board Chair and Chief Executive Officer (CEO). The simultaneous promotions were not coincidental-Reinemund had said he would only take the job if Indra came on board as his second in command. "I can't do it unless I have you with me," she recalled him telling her, according to the 'Business Week'.

The statement drove Indra to tears and she was quick to accept the offer. Together, Indra and Reinemund formed one of corporate America's most unusual but successful management teams what with Reinemund's operational experience and Indra's strategic, "big-picture" thinking. Says Brock H. Leach, the head of Pepsi's Tropicana Products Inc. unit and a long time colleague of Reinemund, "Steve comes from an operational point of view. Nooyi has a very different background, and that's why the combination works. She brings a lot to the party, things I don't think he'd say he does well."

Few know that when Indra and Reinemund first met, they didn't exactly get along. The two were at opposite ends of the spectrum. There was Reinemund who, according to Craig E. Weatherup, CEO of Pepsi Bottling Group Inc., "always looks like he's ready to go on the cover of 'Gentlemen's Quarterly'," and then there is Nooyi who hums to herself during meetings and dresses in what her friend Gordon J. Davis, president of New York's Lincoln Center for the Performing Arts, calls "business Indian", clothes which can be anything from a flowing scarf to a sari. The two persisted, however, and the results of this unique pairing are there for all to see.

Upon taking over as President and CFO in May 2001, Indra continued to keep the company on track with her strategy, which she summed up as, "For any part of the day, we will have a little snack for you," as quoted by 'Business Week'.

By then, the company was selling a dazzling range of snack foods and beverages, from Mountain Dew to Rice-a-Roni, from Captain Crunch cereal to the Gatorade brand of sports drinks. It also owned the Doritos snacks and Aquafina bottled water which meant, no more was Coke their only competitor. PepsiCo was now competing with everyone, from food giants like Kraft to any start-up with a new drink.

Their path ahead was fairly clear. They had to continue to create innovative mechanisms and products to make the company stay on top. "We're a very good suburban-oriented marketing company," Reinemund had said in this context, but admitted, "That's where we've grown over time but there's a huge opportunity in urban markets."

On the business front, the acquisition of Quaker Oats brought in personal as well as public gratification. "With the acquisition of Quaker Oats we were bang there on the health front, reducing cholesterol. And you know the image of Larry in Quaker Oats, people loved it. When we looked at all this in Quaker Oats, the brand Quaker was as exciting to us as was Gatorade. So the combination of the two sets had this as a win-win situation. When we first started talking to them, other companies were not in play."

PepsiCo then went from this $30 billion mammoth to a company with a health focus, a completely different mix and a much more consistent range of products.

Said Nooyi, "We can now see how we have got a range of products from 'fun for you' to 'better for you' to 'good for you', with beverages, meals, snacks, and we have grown this company deliberately over time. It actually started in 1996. It was the first time we started talking about it. Actually, I would say PepsiCo anticipated it in 1990 when we moved to classifying beverages as liquid refreshing beverages as opposed to carbonated soft drinks. That is when we moved into partnerships with Lipton for tea, with Starbucks for cappuccino and we started moving into juices ourselves. So we started really making the move in 1990, and along with the acquisition of Tropicana and then Gatorade, we really cemented our move into non-carbonated beverages and today we have the number one brand literally in every aspect of non-carbonated beverages. The real thinking on health and wellness started in 1996-1997, but then Steve Reinemund accelerated it when he took over and now, you know, it's squarely in focus."

So what did this mean for PepsiCo, still best known for its carbonated drink and salty snacks? Was Indra devising a strategy whereby the company's entire focus would change from fun snacks to health food? Indra replied with her brand of pragmatism, "I would like it to be 50:50. The problem is that, 'fun for you' today has globally 70% of the business, and that is growing. So as long as that keeps growing, you will never be able to catch up easily unless you do something big. The consumer is saying, don't tell us what to eat, let us decide what to eat. That means, we have to be careful. It's improved 'fun for you'. We can improve 'fun for you', but then, I think there is always a place for those products."

Today, in keeping with this strategy she started implementing years ago, the PepsiCo product portfolio has 70% products that are 'fun for you' and 'better for you', while 30% of the portfolio consists of 'good for you' products. Speaking of the future of this strategy, she has said, "If you ask me about PepsiCo a few years from now I would like to see this 'good for you' have a larger portion of our portfolio. It is going to be a challenge. I tell you why. Not because we can't grow 'good for you', but because 70% of the portfolio is growing still at a rate that is going to make it hard for us to grow 'good for you' to catch up and re-balance this equation. We want to be viewed as not just a lifestyle company that brings a slice of joy to you but also as a nutritionally responsible company. That has been our acquisition trajectory over the last few years and I think all our innovation, our strategic direction is headed that way."

Yet there are often allegations of companies like Pepsi harming people's health. Indra has had a lot to say about this. In the 'Economic Times' she said, "I think one gulab jamun has got six Pepsis in it. It is okay that I consume huge quantities of that. So I think it [Pepsi] has its place in the Indian diet." On the CNBC show, 'Mad Money', she told interviewer Jim Cramer, "I eat a bag of Lays every day. Because, you know, obesity doesn't happen because you eat a bag of Lays every day. Let's think of Lays or Ruffles. What is it? It's a potato, an American farmer-grown potato, right here in the United States, that comes out of the soil from the United States, comes straight into a plant that's in the United States. It's merely sliced, fried, lightly salted and put in a bag. And let me just say something, Jim. There's less salt in a bag of potato chips than there is in a slice of bread. There's less salt in a bag of potato chips. Now, if you keep eating potato chips or any chips and don't exercise and eat all kinds of unhealthy foods beyond that and say, 'I'm obese', there's something wrong, okay?"

"The question is," as Indra said in another interview, "how do you make sure you eat it all in one way?" In other words, how do you ensure people do not end up binging on unhealthy snacks and do eat the healthy ones too. Solving this dilemma is the approach of making each PepsiCo brand available in numerous formats. For instance, explains Indra, "In Quaker, we have a whole range of Quaker snacks -- Quaker bars, Quaker Oatmeal and cookies. We have a fantastic pipeline of products."

Pepsi's product portfolio is a reflection of Indra's strategic success at improving the consumer's health. As she explained on 'Mad Money', "I look at our portfolio and say, 'thank God for us.' I mean, I look at zero calorie SoBe Life Water, I look at G2, half the calorie. I look at these Chinese herbal medicine drinks... These are all incredible products. Naked Juice, the ultimate, good-for-you products; Quaker Oats. I look at all of our products. Stila bars from Mexico, which are whole-grain bars. I look at all this and go, 'Thank God for companies like PepsiCo, which are making a difference to their portfolio and we're providing great tasting products.' People are not going to buy products that taste like cardboard. These are all great tasting products. And we're still reducing salt, reducing sugar, frying our products in hot, healthy oil. I think we're doing a great job at transforming our portfolio, and I wish every food and beverage company was the same."

All of this together constituted Indra's "performance with purpose" strategy for PepsiCo. More than just a strategy, this was a philosophy, and in numerous interviews over the years, Indra has spelt out what it means to her.

"[Performance with purpose is] basically PepsiCo saying that companies can no longer perform and toss costs to society. We believe that the new future is public-private partnerships, where companies feel responsible for society at large. So let me give you an example. If companies use water from the ground, it's important we put the water back. It's important we contribute to energy balance. It's important we contribute to a sustainable family if you're in the agricultural business. It's important that if society has a problem with obesity, rather than say, 'It's not my problem,' you work with the lawmakers, work with the regulators and legislators, with NGOs to say, 'How can we address it?' So our performance with purpose is how can we as a company do better by doing better, and that's really the whole idea of performance with purpose, and that's why I believe shareholders should be thrilled that PepsiCo's in fact building a sustainable corporation, sustainable not just financially but sustainable in terms of being a great citizen of every society in which we participate."

Explaining it in greater detail, Indra says, "Clearly, delivering performance is not negotiable... we want to deliver, for the food and beverage business, industry-leading financial performance. No question about it. Let's talk about purpose. Out of the hundred most powerful economic entities, one-third of them are companies. The largest economic entities in the world. Two-thirds are countries, one-third are big companies. You know the size of big multinationals. I mean I look at our company with a market capital of $100 billion that is pretty significant. So we have a profound influence in society—we shape lifestyles, we shape behaviours, the interactive community. And this is not new. This is what PepsiCo has been doing for the past few years. I think, I am just putting some more shape and direction to it. The purpose part comes in three layers. The first is human sustainability. I feel we have to focus on ensuring people live healthy and live longer. So, before making sure the portfolio has health and wellness products and 'fun for you', I want to accelerate the move to a balanced portfolio globally. The second part is environmental sustainability. Clearly, we want to make the world a better place for our children. So, worrying about the water use, energy use and recyclability, all of that stuff. Again you have to balance very carefully with the profit part of it, and talking about sustainability. So everything cannot happen tomorrow. We want to lay out a programme and deliberately work towards it. And the third part is, for our employees and people sustainability. It is, making sure that PepsiCo is the most diverse and the most inclusive place for all people—women, minorities, irrespective of your ethnic background or nationalities. We want to make PepsiCo the place where the best people want to come and work. They feel they can have a great career and progress. Because we are drawing people from communities. We want to be able to work with the local communities and make sure that local communities feel great about having PepsiCo in their neighbourhood.

"So, clearly, I think if PepsiCo could take the leadership on these three purpose-driven activities, we could be among the defining corporations because we would have a clear plan for each one, but we are not going to give up on performance. So, that is the plan and that is what we are going to work against. I think that even in these early days, we have not unveiled this whole strategy globally, just talking to a few of our employees it resonates. Today's is a war for talent. People don't come into the company and stay for reasons other than compensation. Compensation becomes the great leveller. I think if people do not want to come in and stay because they love coming to work every day, I don't think you can hold on to that business. PepsiCo is what it is because of the culture we have. Getting the right people and then retaining them becomes more important than anything else."

Indra also explains what she hopes to achieve through this strategy: "I think PepsiCo has this unique opportunity to be what I would call the defining corporation of the 21st century. When Roger Enrico took over in 1996-1997, we all sat down and we said what is it going to take to make PepsiCo a defining corporation in the 21st century? What do we mean by that? So, let's talk about what we mean by defining corporation and let us talk about what we can do. We started off saying when people talk about the last two decades of the 20th century and talk about the great companies, they talk about IBM, Johnson & Johnson and GE and, you know, names like Microsoft immediately come to mind. But I think, in the first part of the 21st century, and I say first part because I don't want to say 21st century—that is a 100 years, who knows who is going to be around or what the world is going to look like—so the first two or three decades of the 21st century, there is a unique opportunity for PepsiCo to be among the defining corporations. Not "the" but "among the..." because we are going to deliver performance with purpose."

Today, PepsiCo is listed in the New York Stock Exchange and has the highest PE (Price to Earning Ratio) in the food and beverage space and amongst the highest in the CPG (Consumer Packaged Goods) space. Indra says, "That is good news and bad news because there is no place to go but down if you make a mistake. We got to sustain that very high level of performance. We are proud of where we are and I think the people at PepsiCo really would like to keep us there."

Indra attributes a lot of Pepsi's success to its employees. She believes that a company remains great when there is a strong competitor, like Coke, and if you have no competition, a company will atrophy. Both she and Reinemund have consistently tried to balance and integrate work and the home. They have had their children over in office and have encouraged a culture of support. Nooyi has a unique formula that keeps her work-life balance. She feels that you must have an extended family at work to give you that balance.

At PepsiCo, she has ensured that employees actually balance life and work. She views PepsiCo as an extended family and everybody at the company is there to help in every way possible.

Finally, Indra says, "Performance with purpose has energised the company. It has tapped into the emotions of people. The human sustainability, the whole issue of transforming the portfolio: this journey we started six-seven years ago is picking up steam, and we are shifting the portfolio to a nice combination of treat-for-you to good-for-you products."

"In the area of environmental sustainability, our goal is that by 2015, globally, we want to reduce water consumption per unit of production by 20 per cent, electricity by 20 per cent and fuel by 25 per cent. The goal is to reduce, reuse and recycle. I am proud to say that at this point, relative to where we want to be, we are ahead of the original plan.

The last part, the whole issue of talent sustainability—how do we make sure that people who come to work at PepsiCo are here not just to make a living, but to have a life—has unleashed the creativity of people. And they have come up with interesting new programmes to make PepsiCo a much more fun place to be."

Indra's strategic success, her passion for doing good and her mother's prayers have yielded phenomenal results. In the three years following her appointment as President in 2001, the company's annual revenues rose 72%, while net profit more than doubled, to $5.6 billion in 2006. In 2002, PepsiCo's total sales grew nearly 7%, boosting the company's annual revenue growth over its historical 6% growth rate. In 2003, the company announced that it was on track to realize its goal of achieving $400 million in synergies by the end of fiscal year 2004. By 2004, Indra Nooyi was the number two executive at the world's number two soft drink maker. Some industry insiders predicted that she would be moved to another area of the company to gain experience running her own business division. They did not realize Indra was in fact soon to be catapulted to the top. Even as one of the few women in corporate America's highest echelons, and the only Indian woman in 2004, Nooyi had an unbeatable attitude: "I'm sure a glass ceiling exists, but it's both transparent and fragile so you can break it." And break it she did!

The best way to predict the future is to invent it.

— *Alan Kay* —

14

BREAKING THE GLASS CEILING

In the September of 2006, a strange thing happened—Indra Nooyi was kicked out of a board meeting. No, it wasn't for her incessant humming during meetings that she claimed calmed her down. Indra—along with co-CFO Michael D White—were kicked out of that meeting so that the PepsiCo board members could discuss which one of the two would go on to become CEO of PepsiCo.

Indra Nooyi, a young girl from Chennai, who grew up rationing her bath water, was being considered to be the first Indian woman to head a multinational corporation of that size. The odds had always been against her, the glass ceiling always high, but here she was, on the brink of all the success her mother had always prayed for.

Mike White, like Indra, was also a PepsiCo veteran, having worked there for over a decade as Vice Chairman and CFO alongside Indra. A graduate of the Ivy League Johns Hopkins University, it was clear that White had as much of a chance to become CEO as Indra. Both had stellar careers prior to and within the company. Both had proved their worth time and again. Both loved music—when they were asked to leave the board meeting, they went to the 'Jersey Boys' musical on Broadway and sang along to all the Frankie Valli songs. Most interestingly, both were close friends and allies.

Which is why when Indra's appointment as Chief Executive Officer and President of PepsiCo was announced on October 1, 2006, the first thing she did was hop on a plane to go and meet White in Cape Cod where he was vacationing.

A 'CNNMoney' piece by senior editor Betsy Morris tells the story best:

"As Nooyi's plane landed on Cape Cod, there was White waiting for her at the airport with a card he'd written to congratulate her. They took a long walk on the beach. Back at his beach house, he played the piano and she sang. Before she left, they went for ice cream. 'Tell me whatever I need to do to keep you, and I will do it,' she told her long time colleague, who was vice chairman at the time. White said he would sleep on it.

"That kind of scene may be rare in the hypercompetitive realm of C-suites, but not at PepsiCo. PepsiCo's three ex-

CEOs, all on good terms with one another, weighed in to help Nooyi keep White on board. She says she asked the board to increase White's compensation to nearly match hers (Nooyi's 2006 compensation: $7.1 million). White was Pepsi's best operations man—the kind of guy who would be indispensable in a downturn. He would be an important advisor. In the end, White decided to stay. When it was his turn to speak to the troops at the meeting the following week to announce Nooyi's appointment, he put it this way: 'I play the piano and Indra sings.' Says Nooyi: 'I treat Mike as my partner. He could easily have been CEO.' At key meetings she makes sure he is seated on her right.

That isn't the way a new CEO usually takes charge, but Indra Nooyi is an entirely different kind of CEO, a product of her native India as well as of PepsiCo's family-values approach to grooming CEOs."

Indra's spirited attitude to her work is clear from this anecdote. Though a self-professed workaholic, she also says, "You must have fun in whatever you do. Your work takes up so much of your life that if you're not having fun, what's the point in it?"

This isn't exactly the kind of work style one expects from the most powerful woman in business ('Fortune' magazine, 2006) and the third most powerful woman in the world ('Forbes', 2008). But this has been her winning strategy for her life. No wonder her good friend Henry Kissinger says, "It's only a matter of time before she is plucked for a big Washington post, possibly a cabinet job." Indra does not deny the possibility—she is in her early fifties and does not believe this will be her last job. "After PepsiCo, I do want to go to Washington," she has said. "I want to give back—to work for no money for four or five years."

For now, though, she has thrown herself into building the company.

Writes Morris:

"Since becoming CEO, she has reorganized PepsiCo to make it less fixated on the US and broadened the power structure by doubling her executive team to 29. She has installed an Italian native, Massimo d'Amore, atop the division that includes the troublesome US soft drink business, and recruited a former Mayo Clinic endocrinologist to head up R&D. Last year she spent $1.3 billion on acquisitions like Naked Juice, a California maker of soy drinks and organic juice. She has created a motto, 'Performance With Purpose', that puts a positive spin on how she wants PepsiCo to do business both at home and abroad."

Adversaries underestimate Indra at their peril. Financial professionals on the other hand greatly admire her strengths and her focus. Andrew Conway, a beverage analyst with Morgan Stanley Dean Witter, noted, "Indra is extraordinarily financially detailed.... With Tropicana, she was willing to take a lower-return-on-asset business because she saw a way to improve it to get strong margin growth. Her ability to find value in an acquisition is very high."

"If you look at the job entirely from the American perspective, then it becomes impossible to run a global business," says Henry Kissinger, who is a consultant for Pepsi and other companies on international matters. "You have to relate your interests to the interests of other parts of the world, to be relevant in their societies. Indra seems to understand this instinctively."

Just as in her youth, Indra continues to have high standards, not just for herself but for every single person working in her company. In her drive for perfection, she can be a task master. She owns pens in many colours—red, green, and purple—and uses them liberally to mark up everything that crosses her desk. "My scribbles are legendary," she says with a twinkle. "Like, 'I have never seen such gross incompetence.' Or, 'This is unacceptable,' and I underline 'unacceptable' three times." She's joking, but she gets her point across. One of her so-called love letters once scared some secretaries so badly that she had to go to assure them that their bosses were not about to lose their jobs.

These qualities have combined to make Indra a clear winner in the cutthroat corporate world of America.

Just how cutthroat is it? That can be seen in how quickly market situations change, almost completely unpredictably.

When Indra was focusing on healthy foods, PepsiCo found itself back in the cola wars, with Coke's resurgence. With its lower costs and newly acquired brand, Vitaminwater, Coke had once again become a real threat to Pepsi, although it was countering Coke with its new, lower-calorie Gatorade called G2. The corporate rivalry makes Nooyi touchy: "From my perspective, we are a different company... different from a business makeup, different culturally, in the way we think, the way we act. We are different every which way. So if people want to compare us, go right ahead. Is Coke going to have some tailwinds because of [the weak dollar] and the beverage business? Sure. But more power to them. The point is, we are in businesses that give you more good-for-you products, and that means closer to crops. When you're closer to crops, you're going to have some inflation. Am I going to regret it? No, I'm proud of the fact we made the transition."

Regardless of her optimistic stance, the fact remains that the times continue to test Indra, and she is continually challenged to calibrate her vision thinking for a tougher climate, when resources cost more, customers are cautious and the long-running cola wars are far from settled.

Yet, the statistics are testimony to Indra's brilliance: The company's stock has more than doubled since 2003 and now hovers around $70 a share, up about 10% since she took over. In the fourth quarter of 2007, revenue went up 17%, to $12.3 billion, and operating profits rose 9%, to $1.7 billion. Industry analysts at Bank of America say PepsiCo "is demonstrating great flexibility in a tough environment."

Betsy Morris further presents a quick comparison between PepsiCo before and after Indra, and the contrast is clear as day: "PepsiCo today has a completely different flavour. Old Pepsi: Fritos and Cheetos. New Pepsi: Stacy's Simply Naked (pita chips) and Flat Earth (fruit and veggie chips). Old Pepsi: Diet Pepsi and Mountain Dew. New Pepsi: Naked Juice and IZZE Sparkling Clementine. Old Pepsi: ill-fitting acquisitions like North American Van Lines and Wilson Sporting Goods. New Pepsi: joint ventures with compatible partners like Lipton (bottled ice teas) and Starbucks (canned frappuccino)."

●

This tiger in the board room, despite all her professional successes, is in touch with her real priorities. Although million-dollar deals and global business is a daily affair for her, she still primarily considers herself her household's caregiver. She once told the BBC that she calls her mother in India twice a day. "At the end of the day," said the CEO, "don't forget that you're a person, don't forget you're a mother, don't forget you're a wife, don't forget you're a daughter." When your job is done, "what you're left is family, friends, and faith."

PepsiCo has 160,000 employees in 190 countries and is in the midst of transforming into more than a soft drink company. And yet here's what keeps its CEO up at night: "My kids. I worry about my kids." She worries about being available when they want her and about giving the right set of values as she imbibed in her childhood. So, whatever her profile in the outside world, at home she follows the traditional practices she was raised with, like taking off her shoes before entering the puja room. She has developed a natural ability to blend her high-powered career with her Hindu heritage, and her children are surely benefiting from it. As she says, "When I first started in my summer job, I didn't have money to buy business suits. So you just wear a sari, because that is a necessity and it did just fine. What I would not do is flaunt my Indian-ness by wearing a sari to work every day, because it distracts from the job. So, I would not do that. When in Rome do as the Romans do. Social events are different. If I feel comfortable in a sari for a social event, I wear it. You know, a lot is written about 'how she shows up at board meetings in the sari'. My God, I have never worn a sari to board meetings; people play it out in different ways. I think I have never shied away from the fact that I am an Indian and I don't intend to, but you can be at home with both cultures."

•

Is that the secret to her success? Her answer to that is that everyone just tries to do a job but if they pick the right husband then their life becomes much easier. "You know, people like us get very lonely, because you cannot share too much with other people. So you come home and he is there and you can discuss anything with him and he gives you sound advice. Not telling you what to do, he will help you think through all sides of the issue, so that you can make informed decisions. So that way he has been a great support. I would say in terms of balancing the rest of my family, I am an okay mother. I would not say great. I am not available to my kids all the time.

"I have been watching television here (in India) and I have watched the stereotypical Indian mother, running about for the kids' snack for the evening. Really wonderful images of my mother and I am saying to myself, oh my God, my kids have never seen that side of a mother. So I feel bad for them at times, but you know what, they have seen some other kind of mother. I am sure they miss one kind of a mother at some time, but I hope they are proud of this other mother.

"I think to be a CEO is a calling. You should not do it because it is a job. It is a calling and you have got to be involved in it with your head, heart and hands. Your heart has got to be in the job, you got to love what you do, it consumes you. And if you are not willing to get into the CEO job that way, there is no point getting into it. And I love the job, I love the company, I love the people, I loved it when I was president and love it as much as CEO. I want to make something even bigger of this company than it was and what I have to do is decide every moment in time whether I am going to be a mother or a wife or an executive. It's a day to day thing. Although, there are days when I have to go to the school. I do it, but I won't do it every month as they expect mothers to do. I would like to go to see my daughter playing a basketball game. I won't go to every game, but I would to some of them. Everything is a balancing act." With so much to do in twenty four hours, no wonder Indra sleeps only four hours a night. "I feel if I slept six, I would be a basket case."

Her children's positive attitude has helped along the way. It is not unusual, for instance, to find her nine year-old daughter in the office doing homework or having an after-school fireside chat with the then eighty-one year-old founder, Don Kendall. When Indra was travelling, her daughter would call the office to ask for permission to play Nintendo. The receptionist knew the routine and would ask, "Have you finished your homework? Have you had your snack? Okay, you can play Nintendo for half an hour." She would then leave a voice message for Nooyi telling her she had given Tara permission to play Nintendo. This showcases how helpful the culture at PepsiCo is.

The family woman at home understands the importance of building her professional family right too. To keep a company running at top speed, you need to attract the best employees. And according to Indra, this has been PepsiCo's greatest strength. They have created a work environment to attract the best people. Here, employees can actually balance life and work. She views PepsiCo as an extended family. "I love this company. We have an outstanding group of people at Pepsi. The thing I like about PepsiCo is the team that has been built, the culture that exists, a sort of ownership culture. It is extraordinary. I think that's what makes the difference. I always tell my people that what I never want to do is, if they get a competing offer from some other company, to match it and then hold on to them. At that point, I have lost their hearts. When a head hunter calls, I don't want to take the call. I want to say, I love this company so much that I won't take the call. That's what we need to do. Because ultimately it is the people that are going to make or break the company, it is not the assets, it is not the brand."

Indra knows that employees are happy when their families are happy. She throws dinners for members of her team and their spouses, including Q&A sessions in which she insists on getting questions from the spouses and won't sit down until she does. She appreciates the support from her team's families because her career has been tough on her own family. For instance, she says that for a long time she woke up each morning feeling "guilty about everything." Because of her career, her husband had to leave a career at Hewlett-Packard that he loved and work as a consultant. "He helps me. He supports me. He's a man with a big heart," she says. Her incessant travel affected her eldest daughter, and Nooyi regrets this. So she was overjoyed when she heard Preetha, now twenty-four and "my biggest critic" tell a friend recently, "Well, big companies are bad, but I beg to differ about PepsiCo." On long trips, Nooyi calls frequently to keep in touch. On domestic trips, she'll do practically anything to get home at night to be there for breakfast. During an especially tough week last month she received the following e-mail at work from fifteen year-old Tara: "You need to sleep Mom! This is ridiculous! If you plan to do well in Davos then you need to sleep!"

That this is the job Indra Nooyi was born to do is evident in this byte from one of her many interviews: "[If I wasn't working at PepsiCo] I would be applying for a job to come to PepsiCo! I feel like I am home. I'm serious when I say that I would be trying to be part of a company like PepsiCo or trying to change the environment in some other company so it looks more like PepsiCo."

Sare jahan se achcha Hindustan hamara
(Better than the whole world is this India of ours)
— Mohammed Iqbal —

15

INDIA AND INDRA

Being a successful, wealthy Indian living abroad doesn't always come with accolades. Indians who choose to live outside their country are often accused of having taken the easy way out, or of turning their back on their country. But anyone familiar with Indra's life, her struggles and her work would not dare make these accusations against her.

Although Indra became an American citizen in 1988, India and the city of Chennai have remained at the core of this corporate leader's heart. Indra is not one of those NRIs who rarely, if ever, come to India. She and her family make frequent visits and can often be spotted at the annual Chennai music festival, where they quickly become the centre of attention. Indra has always ensured that her daughters, despite being raised in the US, learn the traditions and customs she and her siblings were raised with. And for this she has made sure the family has never drifted too far from their roots.

Cementing this relationship, Indra recently bought a house in Poes Garden, one of Chennai's most posh areas and also home to Chief Minister Jayalalitha. The Nooyis' home is a 4,000 sq ft apartment with an estimated price tag of $1.7 million (about Rs 6.8 crore). The four-flat project was designed to meet Vaastu guidelines, further evidence of Indra and her family's strong Indian connection.

Sentiments aside, India is important to Nooyi from a business perspective as well. As she candidly said in a 2008 interview with 'Businessworld', "India is clearly a star in our portfolio. It is a big bet market for us. The demographics are very favourable. The investment climate is becoming very attractive. We are committed in a significant way to India. The performance of Indian business in the first half of this year, both on the beverage and snacks sides, has been among the highest in our overall portfolios."

Currently, hardly a fraction of PepsiCo's wide product range is available in India. So bringing the whole product range to India is in itself a wonderful business opportunity and one of Nooyi's professional priorities. "India is important to us, not just in terms of profit generation, returns, or growth. India is important to us in a couple of key ways. One, it's a long-term investment market and we would like to participate in growth. We would like to bring all of PepsiCo's products into India and the company will perform with purpose in

India."

But India is more than just a profitable market for the company. Having been raised and educated in Indian universities, Indra also has a unique insight into the Indian manager's psyche. "The Indian management team is really the feeder group for global management. We have got 40 Indian executives who are in PepsiCo senior jobs in the top 400. We really got great Indian executives who are feeding the company." And why is this? "Many of our business heads keep looking for people who have had experience in India to come and run other countries and be functional heads. They can function in any economy because they made it in India where there are many challenges from the infrastructure point of view. And one of the things they learn in India is to get by without much, and do things the low-cost way... And the ingenuity of Indian people is something that you cannot find elsewhere in the world."

Finally, India is more than just a consumer of its American-made products. PepsiCo has gone local in India in a big way, with brands like Kurkure, for instance, which are now being tested in other markets. Says Indra, "Kurkure... has gone to places like Pakistan and is exported to several countries. Now the US is looking at bringing in Kurkure and it may not go with the same spicy flavour, but the substrate with that crisp bite with little bit different flavours could find its way into the US markets soon. So we are working through all of these things and it's a great feeder group for all that technology innovation."

Indra may use business terminology like "feeder group" to describe her country, but in her heart the feelings are purely emotional. The CEO still wears a sari to formal events, dresses up her business suits with an Indian shawl, and on her forehead can often still be seen the mark of *vibhuti,* the sacred ash applied after prayers.

Among PepsiCo's lesser known contributions in India is its work on the development of Indian agriculture. When Indra joined Pepsi, there was a lot of work on the agricultural export side. Today, in India, inclusive growth, that is, how to create jobs in rural areas, is receiving a lot of attention. Says Indra, "Pepsi has, is, and will continue to play a very important role in this whole area. So, let's talk about it. As you said, when we first came in, we did lot of work in Punjab on chillies, tomatoes, and improving yields. It helped the farmers. It helped the farmers hugely, I think it created bumper crops in Punjab of chillies and tomatoes, then they started exporting a whole bunch, and so we had a major export for the food product outside of India. We are now helping farmers to set up citrus crops, right in Punjab again. So, we are doing a tremendous amount of work, helping farmers, improving crop yield, improving harvesting methods, and then helping sell the output of the farm. So I think we have been very, very good citizens and all you have to do is go to Punjab and talk to the chief minister there and I think he will tell you honestly what he thinks about PepsiCo and what we have done for India."

Benefit is always double sided. As farming becomes less and less economical in the west, it makes business sense to get farm products from places like India. Says Nooyi, "I think this booming market alone can absorb a lot of produce. I mean just look at the potato farming we do here for our

Frito Lay products. I think we are a major contributor to the agriculture sector. The more our products draw from natural fruits and vegetables, the more we are going to be helping farming in India."

In her native state of Tamil Nadu as well, a PepsiCo project is helping local economy flourish: "I will tell you, it is more than just agriculture products for our consumption. I do not know how much has been written about the seaweed project down in Rameshwaram. I think it is an incredible project, for which I really think Pepsi deserves a lot of credit. We have gone to a part of the country where the economy is very poor. A lot of women are unemployed there, as is the case in many towns. Pepsi set up a place where they can collect the seaweed, right where they live, in the fishing areas. We don't really need seaweed. But, we take the seaweed, we extract from that carrageenan, which is used in food products, and then we sell it to companies that need the carrageenan. Truly, we don't need it, but we are doing it more as a social responsibility activity to really help that economy. The project is doing us very proud, with good support from the Tamil Nadu government. We were supposed to go down to Tuticorin to see the seaweed project. It would have been an interesting experience by itself. PepsiCo is doing some wonderful things in the country."

•

In 2003, long before Indra was appointed CEO, Pepsi went through bad times when the Indian media was agog with reports that the company was consuming excessive groundwater from Indian villages, leaching their already parched resources. Worse still, the villagers claimed that PepsiCo, along with rival Coca Cola, were allowing the pesticides from the local groundwater to remain in the locally manufactured Pepsi. Along with then CEO Steve Reinemund, Indra and the rest of the company braced themselves as riots of protestors smashed Pepsi bottles on Indian streets and the press was plastered with images of angry, exploited villagers. Indra was livid and indignant, "For somebody to think that Pepsi would jeopardize its brand—its global brand—by doing something stupid in one country is crazy."

In every interview, at every forum, at any opportunity, Indra rose to the defence of her company, whose products she and her children regularly consumed: "First of all, let me reiterate and say without a shadow of doubt, our products are the safest in the world and whether the product is of New York or Beijing or Delhi or Shanghai or Thailand or Australia, it is the same product and uniformly safe. So, the safety of our products is not in question at all. So, let me pass that thing on the side. I think, if I sit back and look at what's happened in India, I think the NGO really wanted to highlight the issue of food safety standards for India. I think that whole controversy started with milk. A lot of pesticides in milk and not much was done with the first study that was done and so, Coke and Pepsi got into the spot. Again, I am not going to second guess what the NGO was doing. The fact of the matter is we were caught in cross lines. When you are testing a very complex finished beverage with a testing method which is really not geared towards testing these sorts of products, we many times get false positive results."

"Now, the government has since tested many, many samples of Coke and Pepsi. We have tested our own samples of Pepsi from around the world and I can tell you, we have no pesticides in our products because we test every input, where there are reliable tests for inputs, which are simple. We test every input that goes into Pepsi and unless those inputs pass very rigorous quality standards we never put them into the product. So again, I personally stand by the safety of our products."

"Having said that, try explaining false positive results to the public! The fact of the matter is the public has been told that there are some low levels of pesticides probably in soft drinks. Nobody focuses on the low level; they focus on pesticides in the soft drinks. Our brand is under attack. We have to do something about it."

"So, what did we do? First, we have to find the testing methodology, which does not exist in the world because nobody tests that level. We are talking about one drop of pesticide in the Olympic-sized swimming pool of water that is what we are talking about, right. Let's be honest about what we are talking about. So, we have to find first a testing protocol to test at that level. It has taken us three years. We think we have a method, but the problem is the testing methods to test at that level are very expensive. What is the point of having a testing method when you can't test all the samples on a repetitive basis?"

"But, I have a second bigger issue. Is this about food safety standards for the country or about only soft drinks? Now, we have to really talk about this because I think the issue is food safety standards across the nation. So where I do agree with the CSE (Centre for Science and Environment) and the NGOs is that I think they are all a labour of love—all NGOs. They are after the right thing—food safety standards. So, let's help them address the issue of food safety standards and let's not get unduly caught up in the fashion we were caught in the past. Then we look at NGOs and say they are good for democracies, they are good for India. How many helped them fulfil their purpose of having food safety standards? So, we work with the government to put in safety standards for all food products and we will help by helping the government set up the food testing laboratories. We are happy to do that. But the government has to decide what standard can be tested and what levels should exist for products in the entire food chain, not just our products."

In its efforts to arrive at the best food health policies, PepsiCo soon set up a system of participation with NGOs, on which Indra said, "On the health and wellness issue, we are talking to NGOs around the world, constructively talking about the issue we are trying to address. We are trying to address obesity as an issue. Let us talk about calories in and calories out; because what causes obesity is not the eating habits, it's a sedentary lifestyle that is causing obesity. There is no point saying, I am going to tell you what to eat and what not to eat, but incidentally that means you can sit in front of the television longer. This doesn't solve the issue. You have got to figure out how to get these people moving, how to get them exercising more. We need to work on it. So, when we work with NGOs, what we are trying to talk about is family balance. Let's talk about not banning products in school, because kids are going to bring it later on. Let's talk about how to give them nutrition education. Let's talk about how to get them working, so we are big participants in programmes like 'America On The Move', where we get people to pedometers and say go up there and walk the steps. So we want the people to work holistically on issues. When we work with NGOs and engage with them, we don't engage with them on their one-sided attack of companies like us. We try to find out what are the underlying issues they are trying to address and then approach them in terms of how to address those issues holistically as opposed to just picking on manifestation of the issue."

Indra also appreciated the anxiety many Indians felt, "Parents were scared that their children were consuming things they had never consumed. And now they had a reason to stop it. Pesticides in cola. Nobody stopped to say, 'What pesticides? Or, incidentally, your tea and your coffee has many thousand times that.'"

Indra presented a more than convincing argument, and eventually the whole issue blew over. Even so, she believes she made a critical error during the pesticide controversy: "One thing I should have done was appear in India three years ago and say, 'Cut it out. These products are the safest in the world, bar none. And your tests are wrong.'" She has often said that perhaps if she had been CEO at the time, her actions would have been a lot different and she would have been on the first plane to India, representing not just her company but as an Indian and a consumer of PepsiCo's products. But the past cannot be undone, and Indra has gone on to more than redeem herself, her company and its products.

The woods are lovely, dark and deep. But I have promises to keep, and miles to go before I sleep, and miles to go before I sleep.

— *Robert Frost* —

16

MILES TO GO

And so we have Indra Nooyi, the pride of two countries, two universities, two daughters, but of one woman in particular—her mother Shantha, whose countless hours of prayer and childhood exercises in delivering speeches on world issues set the foundation for Indra to head one of the world's largest conglomerates.

Indra's journey has not been an easy one. She has had to combat discrimination both for being an Indian and for being a woman in corporate America. Indra took on the job with the same aggression and doggedness she brings to all her work.

For this, she has sometimes been harshly criticised. For instance, a 2005 speech she gave to the graduates of the Columbia University Business School received much flak. In the speech, she compared the five fingers of the human hand to the five continents. America, she said, was like the middle finger—the longest and strongest of all the fingers, which could reach out to others most easily, but if this were not done carefully, it could be misinterpreted as a rude gesture. This she said was the fate of America in global trade—a tendency to be seen as rude when all it was doing was reaching out. Through this analogy, which proved to be unpalatable to many who heard and read the speech later, Indra warned the fresh graduates to ensure that they didn't inadvertently present an incorrect picture of America in their international business dealings.

Perhaps it wasn't the most delicately put message, but this is Indra for you—outspoken, blunt, perhaps a bit brash, but capable of getting her point across loud and clear. And the minute she realized she had ruffled feathers, she did not think twice about issuing an immediate public apology, with no shame or embarrassment.

It is this straightforward, passionate style that Indra has infused in PepsiCo as well, and it should be no surprise that it is one of the world's most successful conglomerates. Indra says, "...If you were at PepsiCo and you left PepsiCo and you saw the kinds of people you were working with in the new company, you would realize the power of the PepsiCo people. It is a youthful culture. It is a bunch of 'can do' people. Everybody is eager to sign on to new challenges. They want to be the best of what they do. I don't know what it is... maybe it is the Pepsi they drink."

"Remember the old chimpanzee ad for Pepsi? ... There is an old ad for Pepsi, which I think was the best example of what Pepsi is all about. In this ad a bunch of scientists were feeding Pepsi to a chimp and the other red drink to another chimp. After a few months of Pepsi Diet and red diet, the red diet chimp would utter a couple of words, in a listless way, but the Pepsi chimp was in this convertible with the babes. What that goes to show you is that the Pepsi culture is one where the people are youthful."

"There is a spirit of candor that pervades the whole company... That is what has kept this company growing. It is a Darwinian principle. If you don't like this high performance culture, you leave. In recent days we haven't been losing people. People want to be part of the PepsiCo culture."

Candour, spirit, youth... these are the words that define PepsiCo as well as Indra Nooyi, the straight talking tough lady at its helm. Under her, the company has bravely embraced radical change and experimented with new ideas.

In 2010, for instance, PepsiCo decided not to advertise during the American Super Bowl, the annual championship game of the National Football League (NFL) that companies will spend millions of dollars on. For the first time in almost two decades, PepsiCo did not create ads to beat arch rival Coca Cola and instead chose to spend $20 million on a social media (internet) campaign. This was unheard of, and the strategy attracted both praise and brickbats. Like most things about the company, people either loved it or hated it; there is hardly ever any in between when it comes to this vibrant organization. The 'Pepsi Refresh' campaign (www.refresheverything.com) offers grants of up to $250,000 to anyone—people, businesses or non-profit companies—with the best idea to transform society and initiate social change.

Doesn't this whole idea just scream 'Indra'? And she continues to rock the boat at PepsiCo, be it through her fiery interview sound bytes or by shaking up traditional corporate hierarchies and creating new positions like 'Chief Scientific Officer'.

For her achievements she has received numerous awards and recognitions. For instance, she is consistently named among the holy pantheon that is the 'Forbes' ratings of the world's most powerful people. She consistently figures on lists of most powerful women, people, heads of business, Indians, expatriates and NRIs.

Indra is active in both the wider business community as well as in the public sphere. In business, her commitment is evidenced by her membership of the board of directors of PepsiCo, Inc., serving as a successor fellow at Yale Corporation, as a member of the board of Motorola, the International Rescue Committee and the Lincoln Centre for the Performing Arts in New York City. She is also a member of the Trilateral Commission and on the advisory boards of the Yale School of Management, Planet Finance and Greenwich Breast Cancer Alliance as well as on the board of trustees of the Eisenhower Fellowships and the Asia Society. She has also been recently elected to the board of directors of the Federal Reserve Bank of New York.

For her many professional accomplishments, her strong belief in lifelong learning, and her advocacy of women in business, Pace University conferred upon her the degree of Doctor of Commercial Science, *honoris causa,* with all the rights and privileges pertaining thereunto.

The Indian paper 'India Abroad' named her the Person of the Year 2006, describing her with the following words: "Finally she has proved that it is possible to be a daughter, wife and devoted mother—and yet find the time and space for high achievement. That plays right into the community's cultural ethos that values a woman as homemaker, while increasingly recognizing that she can be much more, do much more in the larger world outside."

"Secondly, and equally importantly, she has proved through personal example that you do not need to hide who you are, pretend to be something you are not, in order to be successful. Indra Nooyi is, first, a grateful daughter, unabashedly eloquent in reiterating how her parents, particularly her mother, instilled in her the virtues she holds most dear, the values that have helped shape her into the achiever she is. She is, next, a wife and mother; clear in her mind that the needs of husband Raj and her two daughters are as important to her as are the needs of the larger family of Pepsi employees whose fate and fortune she oversees."

"Indra Nooyi is American in the energy, enterprise and innovation she brings to her professional life; yet, she manages this without sacrificing the Indianness that is an essential ingredient in her personality. Her saris, her prayers are all the stuff of legend, an image of Ganesha has pride of place on her work table, and visitors are as apt to be drawn into a discussion of the elephant-headed god's place in Hindu iconography as into discussing the best practices of business.

"For a community caught between two positions—to stay true to your heritage, or to assimilate, to merge, with the culture of the adopted land—Indra Nooyi is the perfect example; her life, her achievements, indicating that the highest accomplishment is possible without sacrificing who, and what, you are."

These are fitting words to describe Indra Nooyi, who has created history and whose achievements have served as a beacon for anyone with a dream. But this is only the beginning for her. Indra is in her fifties, with many active years of work before her. What you have read so far is a chronicle of the first part of her life and work—there are certainly still many achievements ahead of her and the world looks forward to these.

Epilogue

She adjusted the brightly coloured shawl draped over the right sleeve of her dark business suit as she took a sip from her glass of ice cold Pepsi. Cradling the telephone between her right ear and shoulder, she heard the interviewer, Feroz Ahmed from 'Businessworld' magazine, clear his throat. He was calling her long distance from New Delhi, India, in her office in Purchase, New York. It was late evening and she was eager to get home to her daughters, but daily interviews were part of her responsibilities as CEO and she was giving it her best.

"Indra, thanks for taking my call, I know it's pretty late in New York, so this is going to be my last question," said Ahmed.

"No problem, Feroz, just doing your job," Indra replied with a smile in her voice. "Go ahead."

"What do you want your legacy to be whenever you leave PepsiCo?"

Indra paused to think and took another sip of her drink. Then she began to speak.

"I think about this often. Whenever I leave PepsiCo, looking back I want people to say that in the first part of the 21st century, if you look at the defining corporations of the world, PepsiCo was one of them because PepsiCo was a good company—good in the commercial as well as in the moral sense. And PepsiCo set the standard for what a good corporation should be."

Indra Nooyi has certainly set the standard for what a good daughter, wife, mother and CEO should be.